The Rainbow Bridge: Pet Loss Is Heaven's Gain

Pet Loss From A Christian Perspective

Niki Behrikis Shanahan

Author Of

There Is Eternal Life For Animals
and
Animal Prayer Guide

Published By:

Pete Publishing
Tyngsborough, Massachusetts

We Welcome You To Visit Us At:

www.eternalanimals.com

The Rainbow Bridge:
Pet Loss Is Heaven's Gain

First Published 2007

ISBN-10 Digit: 097203014X
ISBN-13 Digit: 9780972030144

Library of Congress Control Number: 2007925172

Published By:

Pete Publishing
P. O. Box 282
Tyngsborough, MA 01879

www.eternalanimals.com

The photos in this book are not the actual story characters unless stated.

Acknowledgments

I wish to thank the following people for their assistance in making the book *The Rainbow Bridge: Pet Loss Is Heaven's Gain* possible:

Jesus Christ, our Lord and Savior, who made the salvation, eternal life, healing, and help for mankind and animals possible. If this book is helpful and beneficial to anyone, it is due to the guidance and knowledge given to me by the Good Shepherd.

Thank you to Sylvia Corbett, Cover Illustrator, for her beautiful artwork. She has given us a glimpse into the Heavenly entrance that awaits our beloved animal companions. Sylvia is a Christian animal lover from California. She is a Graphic Designer for The King's College and Seminary at The Church on the Way in Van Nuys, California.

I'd like to thank Susie Meskell from Nevada for all her help in proofreading the manuscript. Susie is a Christian animal lover with two cats, Spider and Panda. Her beautiful dog, Bambie, now resides in Heaven.

My husband, Jack, for all his vital Technical Support that make our publications and website possible. This includes assistance with manuscript layout, e-book conversions, inventory spreadsheets, and every aspect of day-to-day computer maintenance. He is a committed Prayer Partner for all our website prayer requests, has a real heart for all animals and a strong love for the Lord. Jack is a significant part of this ministry, and a great blessing to me.

Reviews For

The Rainbow Bridge: Pet Loss Is Heaven's Gain

I was excited to hear that Ms. Shanahan had a new book release. I have had the pleasure to read and review her two former works, *There Is Eternal Life For Animals* and *Animal Prayer Guide*, and I was truly the one who was blessed. As I settled down to read her new work, I knew this too would be a blessing to me and I was not disappointed.

In her new work, *The Rainbow Bridge: Pet Loss Is Heaven's Gain*, our author again takes us through Biblical proof that our beloved pets are indeed waiting for us on the other side. As always, her research is concise and conclusive, and leaves you with the reassurance that God truly is taking care of our beloved pets.

However, she goes into some new veins in this work such as sharing how pets were companions throughout history. I found this information to be so interesting that I reread it several times. And I absolutely loved Chapter three, "Encouraging and Miraculous Stories." These stories warmed my heart and uplifted me for days. Wonderful. She goes on in Chapter Four to discuss what the Bible says about life after death, Chapter Five deals with overcoming depression and she gives you some helpful advice and aids to implement to help lessen the blow of your loss.

In Chapter 6 she encourages us to look to the future. It is a great feeling and brings much comfort to know that your pet is being well taken care of, and is eagerly waiting to be reunited with you. And her final chapter is given to a Memorial Service that you can hold for your pet, allowing you a way of closure for your loss, and respect to the pet you love.

As far as this reviewer is concerned I strongly feel that Ms. Shanahan should be given a standing ovation for the work she has done in the awareness that our passing pets are certainly part of our future. She has felt the very pulse of grieving pet owners and carefully applied healing ointment to help mend the broken heart, and bring hope and peace through her writings.

Her new book is yet just another cooling balm to sooth the troubled soul. I cannot encourage you enough to read every one of her excellent books; you will never be the same. Thank you, Ms. Shanahan, from the owner of many beloved pets who I know are waiting for me on the other side. I am sure in Heaven when they hear your name, they smile.

Rev. Shirley Johnson, Florida
Senior Reviewer, MidWest Book Review

"For anyone who has ever lost a beloved pet companion, *The Rainbow Bridge: Pet Loss Is Heaven's Gain* by Niki Behrikis Shanahan is a source of comfort, hope and encouragement that the reader will want to revisit again and again during the difficult days ahead.

While reading this wonderful book, you will come away with the feeling that Ms. Shanahan is sitting right there beside you, sharing in your pain and sorrow, as she relates to you the inspiring true story of her own personal loss and redemption after the passing of her beloved cat, Pete.

Give this book to anyone who has lost a pet, and you will be giving them a two-fold blessing: Not only will they will receive the peace and assurance of knowing with certainty that their pets are in the presence of God and that someday they will be re-united with them again in Heaven, but they will also learn of God's loving plan to help them overcome the devastating pain and depression that accompanies the loss of a pet.

Ms. Shanahan's book shows us many wonderful and special ways that we can forever memorialize our pets while at the same time offering us the strength and courage to one day love again."

Annie Mals, President,
The Peaceful Kingdom Alliance 4 Animals, CA

"Your new book is very special! It gives those who are grieving over the loss of a beloved pet, the comfort and assurance that they will be together again in Heaven. You also show how to move through the grieving process. So many of us were taught that animals just return to the dust, and it is wonderful to have proof from Scripture that animals do live on with us in Heaven. Thank you for giving us this knowledge and hope for our beloved pets."

Frances Weber
President & Founder, The Ark, South Carolina

"This is a wonderful, promising book to read, especially for those who are grieving over the loss of their loving pets, as I am. The information will assure you that, by God's own words and promise, your pet is now safe and healthy up in Heaven, waiting for you."

Susie Meskell, Nevada

Table of Contents

Chapter 1

Introduction

To live in hearts we leave behind
Is not to die.
Thomas Campbell

Your beloved animal companion has passed on. However, they are not really dead – they have entered God's presence. They now reside in Heaven where they will live forever in perfect health, happiness, and peace. Now you must look to the future for your reunion with them, where you will never be separated again. I like the way the hymnist, John Newton, put it in his song Amazing Grace:

> "When we've been there ten thousand years, Bright shining as the sun, We've no less days to sing God's praise, Than when we first begun."

No less days. There will be no end to our happy life with them in Heaven.

In this book I want to show you how to overcome the painful experience of losing your precious pet. As you read, you will see that we were all created to be eternal beings. There is a better life ahead for all of us, and God wants to help you in every aspect of your life. God cares about you! Jesus said, "In this world you will have trouble, but take heart! I have overcome the world."[1] He also said that He doesn't want us to be troubled or afraid.[2]

Heaven is a very real place! In order to give you a better insight into what awaits us in Heaven, I want to share a couple

---

[1] John 16:33, NIV
[2] John 14:27

of quotes from a book called ***Intra Muros,*** written in 1898 by Rebecca Ruter Springer. Rebecca, a devout Christian, had a vision of Heaven while she lay in bed near death. This is a century-old near-death experience. The following is from a conversation that she had with her brother-in-law in Heaven.

> "If only we could realize while we are yet mortals, that day by day we are building for eternity, how different our lives in many ways would be! Every gentle word, every generous thought, every unselfish deed, will become a pillar of eternal beauty in the life to come. We cannot be selfish and unloving in one life, and generous and loving in the next; the two lives are too closely blended – one but a continuation of the other." Rebecca states in her preface of the book, "I may be able to partly tear the veil from the death we so dread, and show it to be only an open door into a new and beautiful phase of the life we now live."

> Springer, Rebecca Ruter. ***Intra Muros.*** David C. Cook Publishing Company, 1898.

When my husband and I lost our beloved cat, Pete, we were devastated. He was so wonderful and such a joy to be with! We often called him "The Baby." We adopted Pete when he was 8 years old, and in 2001 he went to Heaven at age 21. It was very painful, there were many tears, and today I still miss him so very much. I think of him every day. The passing of a loved one is something that we are never going to get used to, but time does ease the pain of our temporary separation.

Please know that you are not alone. People all over the world experience the painful loss of a loved one at one time or another. One such example is Michael, a Massachusetts state trooper. His partner, Granite, a 2 ½ year old black Labrador, was struck and killed by a car at the start of the Boston Marathon. Granite had bolted from Michael's car before he could leash the K-9. Michael was so distraught at the scene that his wife drove there immediately to console him. Michael said, "I don't think there are any words that can explain the loss. Some people say it's your partner, but partners go home at the end of your shift, and don't come home and sleep on your pillow, on your bed or at your feet."

How can we bear this loss, and how can we cope? It's times like this that most of us turn to our faith in God to bring us through our grief. We look to our Creator for strength, comfort, and a greater hope for a future life in Heaven. The good news is that He never lets us down! When we look in the Bible we see that God has made provision for our eternal life. And, if we look at the Scriptures closely, we'll see that it includes all the animals! So we should focus on the happiness that the future holds for us when we will be reunited in Heaven.

There are many Scriptures revealing that all the animals go to Heaven, such as Psalms 36:6 which says that God preserves people and animals. None of us are preserved in this life, so it's easy to see that this refers to an afterlife in Heaven. The objective for my book, *There Is Eternal Life For Animals,* is to prove through the Bible that all animals go to Heaven, and the book does accomplish its goal!

You can pray and ask God to give you peace and to soften your grief. Try not to dwell and agonize on the painful memories. Instead, picture your beloved pet in Heaven running around, playing, and having a wonderful time. Channel your thoughts to a beautiful vision of your baby running in fields of flowers, and having fun with all the other animals in Paradise.

A good way to overcome your pain is to help another pet. There are so many beautiful animal companions just waiting for a wonderful parent like you and a happy home! The shelters are filled with them. You can save a life, and they can help to save yours. Animal companions bring so much joy and happiness that it's often hard to decide who's helping whom the most. They'll help to distract you from your loss.

The day after Pete passed away my husband and I were both in the dining room crying and trying to console each other. Suddenly I looked out the window and there was Joey, the stray cat that we had been feeding. He was running down the steep driveway across the street, and he was headed right for our yard! It broke the heart wrenching moment, and turned our attention to someone who needed us.

I immediately went out to see him, and gave him something to eat. Shortly thereafter, we adopted him, and now he's part of our family. Did he take Pete's place? No way! No pet is going to take another one's place. That's not the point in adopting another animal. The point is to create another beautiful bond of love, friendship, and companionship.

Just like parents love each of their children as individuals, so we love each of our animal companions as individuals. God made every creature different with his or her own unique personality.

The first few days after our pet leaves us are the most devastating. I recall when Pete left us that I felt like I was in a trance. Even just before we left the house to try to take Pete to the veterinarian, I was doing things in a trance-like way. We never made it to the veterinarian, because Pete went home to be with the Lord in my arms, in the car on our way there. It's the same as losing a human child for those of us who really love our furry kids. At first you can't even believe that they left. My loss hit me only a couple of months after my Dad went home to be with the Lord in 2001.

For a time, life suddenly becomes empty and painful. Everything reminds us of our pet. We don't know what to do with their belongings, because it hurts to look at them, and yet we don't want to part with them. I put quite a few things away in my closet so that they were out of sight, but still here with me. I felt the need to have Pete's pictures everywhere. I bought special "baby" picture frames, and put his photos in them. There's a mourning process that each person goes through, and everyone handles it a little differently.

On the day that Pete left me, I remember that my friend, Harriet, called me. She didn't call me all that often, so we both knew that the Lord put it on her heart to call because I needed her. When I called and told my mother, she came right over to my house, which is a 45 minute drive, and stayed with us for a couple of hours. Another friend sent flowers, which I thought was very sweet.

I received some condolence cards, too. Thank God for family and friends that care. However, in general, pet loss support is an area that our society has neglected. Unfortunately, we all find out that there are many non-animal lovers who are insensitive whether they mean to be or not. Regrettably, many of these insensitive people are "Christians." All we can do is pray for them, and forgive them for their ignorance.

My intentions are that this book should be uplifting and encouraging, however, I do want you to know that I have been through the same experience that you have been through. I have gone through the same feelings and heartaches that you are going through. So now let's move forward to see how we are going to pull out of our depression and sorrow, while we honor and always remember our beloved animal companions. Understand that we will always miss our pets until we are reunited in Heaven, but until then we must all fulfill our destiny here on earth.

"If I have any beliefs about immortality,
it is that certain dogs
I know will go to Heaven,
and very, very few people."
James Thurber

The Rainbow Bridge

We hear so much about "The Rainbow Bridge" relative to when our beloved animal companions pass from this life into the next life in Heaven. The concept of the Rainbow Bridge originates from the Bible. God told Noah that there was going to be a great flood coming to earth, because everyone was so wicked except for Noah and his family. He told Noah to build an ark with very detailed specifications. He was instructed to put his family and two of each animal, and seven of some others, in the ark with him just before the flood, which destroyed all other living creatures on earth.

After the flood, Noah, his family, and all the animals entered into a covenant with God. A covenant is a promise or an agreement. This covenant was not only made with Noah and his family, but God repeatedly stated that He was entering this covenant with the animals.

Never let anyone tell you that animals are not important to God or that He doesn't love them. Animals are so significant to God that He entered into a special covenant with them, and repeated this fact several times in the Bible. The covenant states that God will never again cut off all life with a flood.

"'I establish My covenant with you: Never again will all life be cut off by the waters of a flood; never again will there be a flood to destroy the earth.' And God said, 'This is the sign of the covenant I am making between Me and you **and every living creature with you**, a covenant for all generations to come: I have set My **rainbow** in the clouds, and it will be the sign of the covenant between Me and the earth. Whenever I bring clouds over the earth and the **rainbow** appears in the clouds, I will remember My covenant between Me and you **and all living creatures of every kind.'"**

"Never again will the waters become a flood to destroy all life. Whenever the **rainbow** appears in the clouds, I will see it and remember the everlasting covenant between God and **all living creatures of every kind on the earth.'** So God said to Noah, 'This is the sign of the covenant I have established between Me **and all life on the earth.'"**[3]

Rev. Kenneth E. Hagin (1917 – 2003) was the pastor and founder of the Rhema Bible Church in Oklahoma. At the age of 15, Hagin had a near-death experience, which resulted from a malformed heart. He wrote about his experience in his book, *I Believe In Visions*.

In the following quote, Kenneth Hagin describes the throne of God that he saw in Heaven. He mentions the rainbow over the throne of God.

---

[3] Genesis 9:11-17, NIV

"Again I saw Jesus about where the top of the tent should be, and I went to Him through the air. When I reached Him, together we continued on to Heaven. We came to the throne of God, and I beheld it in all its splendor. I was not able to look upon the face of God; I only beheld His form."

"The first thing that attracted my attention was the rainbow about the throne. It was very beautiful. The second thing I noticed was the winged creatures on either side of the throne. They were peculiar-looking creatures, and as I walked up with Jesus, these creatures stood with wings outstretched. They were saying something but they ceased and folded their wings. They had eyes of fire set all around their heads, and they looked in all directions at once."

"I stood with Jesus in the midst, about 18 to 24 feet from the throne. I looked at the rainbow first, at the winged creatures, and then I started to look at the One who sat upon the throne. Jesus told me not to look upon His face. I could only see a form of a Being seated upon the throne."

"Jesus talked with me for nearly an hour. I saw Him as plainly as I ever saw anyone in this life. I heard Him speak."

Hagin, Kenneth E. *I Believe In Visions.* Tulsa: Faith Library Publications, 1996, Pages 49-50.

Another reference in Scripture to a rainbow appears in the book of Revelation. It tells of a rainbow around the throne of God. In Revelation Chapter 4 it describes some unusual animal creatures that sound like what Rev. Hagin saw in his NDE of Heaven.

"And the one who sat there had the appearance of jasper and carnelian. A **rainbow**, resembling an emerald, encircled the throne."[4]

You can see that the animals are so important to God that He would make a covenant with them. There are numerous Bible verses that reveal God's love and concern for animals. I have covered this subject more thoroughly in my book, ***There Is Eternal Life For Animals***, Chapter 2, *God's Relationship With The Animals*.

Changes Are Difficult

There's a huge impact upon our lives when a loved one leaves us. It changes our whole world. Most of us don't like changes, especially if we're happy with the way things are. It's a traumatic experience, and it's very painful to go through.

As a general rule, I think that all creatures are a bit resistant to changes. Animals don't like change very much either. For example, before we bought our house, we lived in a very small condo for several years. It was only about 600 sq. feet of luxurious living space! It was quite crowded, and by the time we moved we had two cats, Pete and Luke.

Luke, a former feral cat that we rescued when he was about 6 months old, and he had only been with us for 6 months when we bought our house. At that point, two people and two cats in a small place was really tight and uncomfortable. Tight quarters or not, I had been determined to capture Luke, and adopt him after feeding him and his siblings. This became a priority after two of his siblings were hit by cars. I wasn't going to let this little Cherub get away, and with the Lord's help, I captured him.

---

[4] Revelation 4:3, NIV

When the day came for us to move into our new house, we put Luke in a carrier and carried Pete on my lap as we only had one pet carrier. Driving only a few minutes away from our former home, we put them in a bedroom upstairs with food, water, a litter box, the carrier, and we closed the door. I opened the carrier door, but Luke wanted to stay in there for a while. We wanted to keep them in a safe place while we moved all the furniture, and didn't want them to accidentally get out of the house.

At one point, I thought I'd go in the room and check on them to see how they were doing. I wish I'd had a camera with me. Both cats were in the carrier together. Lukie was in the back and Pete in the front! It was so funny to see them both squished in there, but I'm sure that being together in there seemed to be somewhat of a comfort for them.

Finally, the big move was over, everyone had gone home, the house was quiet, and we opened the door to their room. By the time it became dark outside, Pete and Luke felt more comfortable to venture out of the room, and see what this was all about. Before long they realized that life was improving for them, and discovered that there was a lot more room for them to play in this new place.

In fact, they could run around and chase each other in circles on the first floor, as it's an open floor plan. It's amazing how two cats can sound like a herd of elephants when they're running! Luke, being about a year old at the time, showed no signs of having the upper hand with Pete, who was in his late teens then. Pete would run around the house with Luke, and keep up with him with no problem!

Then they found out that they had a basement they could explore with lots of stuff in it. There were double atrium doors that had windows low enough so they could see their backyard quite well. The front and back doors were fitted with screen doors that also had low windows for their viewing pleasure.

Lukie on the left and Pete on the right, are
sleeping on one of their bay windows.

There were two bay windows on the first floor with wide shelves for them to lounge on in the sun all day with thick scatter rugs for the utmost comfort. Since the house was built with 2 x 6 studs, all the windows have a 6" sill, which is well suited for the cats of the house.

Yes, after that frightening change from the safe and secure environment that they called home, it turned out that it was all for the better, and they were very happy about it!

Someday when we see Heaven with all of its beauty and grace, when we're together with our loved ones, and realize that there's no end to this beautiful dream, we won't care about what we've left behind on earth. All the animals can run freely, and there's never a danger of being hit by a car, being hurt in any way or of them becoming lost. In Heaven there's freedom, and lots of wide-open space to enjoy. These little ones will never be fearful, experience sickness, or be inflicted with any disease again in their everlasting and eternal homes.

Chapter 2

Animals As Companions Through History

According to The American Pet Products Manufacturing Association (APPMA) in 2003-2004 there were 77.7 million cats in homes, 65 million dogs, and 16.8 million small animals. Data shows that 62% of U.S. households have companion animals, and that pet owning has increased by 10 million animals in ten years. Dogs and cats are found in one out of three U.S. households.

In a recent survey of Veterinary Pet Insurance (VPI) policyholders and other pet owners who visited petinsurance.com, 56 percent of those who responded said their pet sleeps right next to them each night. So if you find yourself cuddling up with your furry friends each night when you go to bed, you're not alone.

Has there always been a bond of companionship and friendship between people and animals? Many people have wondered about the history of animals as companions in Bible days.

During 200 BC to 1400 AD cats spread through Europe and Asia with the expansion of the Roman Empire, the silk trade, and Christian and Buddhist missionary movements. By the end of this period, domestic cats could be found from Ireland to Japan. From 1400 AD to present, cats traveled on ships as mousers, and began to cross the seas in the fifteenth and sixteenth centuries. Colonization by European countries brought cats to other continents. By about 1850, cats could be found almost anywhere there were people.

There's an incident in the Bible that reveals something about dogs as pets in those early days. A Syro-Phoenician woman made the statement that even the dogs under the table eat of the children's crumbs.[5] In the book *All The Animals Of The Bible Lands*, G. S. Cansdale points out that the Greek word "kunarion" is found here, which means little dogs. Therefore, we know that there were dogs that were pets in Bible days.

One Bible story that clearly illustrates an animal that was a pet to a dear man is the one which follows. Although it's a sad story, it does illustrate the relationship very clearly. The prophet Nathan tells David a parable in order to show David that he is guilty of sin. David took his neighbor's wife, Bathsheba, and God is using this story as an analogy to bring out the point that David was wrong.

We can learn a few things from this portion of Scripture. What we see here, in addition to David's reprimand, is that God shows compassion and sensitivity to the poor man who lost his pet lamb! The Bible is telling us that this strong, loving relationship, like many people have with their pets, is like a parent-child relationship. There is no implication in the Bible that this type of relationship is unusual. Rather the implication here is that it is acceptable and normal.

The reason that I am pointing this out is because there are some people who belittle and criticize individuals who love their pets in this manner. Not only is there a stamp of approval on this relationship, but the Bible specifically states that the rich man was wrong in taking away the poor man's pet! He compares the poor man losing his pet to a man who loses his wife. Further, David wants the guilty man killed, which equates the value of the lamb to that of a person, since the punishment for the murder of a man is death!

> "The Lord sent Nathan to David. When he came to him, he said, There were two men in a certain town, one rich and the other poor. The rich man had a very large number of sheep and cattle, **but the poor man had**

---

[5] Mark 7:28

nothing except one little ewe lamb he had bought. He raised it, and it grew up with him and his children. It shared his food, drank from his cup and even slept in his arms. It was like a daughter to him."

"Now a traveler came to the rich man, but the rich man refrained from taking one of his own sheep or cattle to prepare a meal for the traveler who had come to him. Instead, he took the ewe lamb that belonged to the poor man and prepared it for the one who had come to him. David burned with anger against the man and said to Nathan, As surely as the Lord lives, the man who did this deserves to die! He must pay for that lamb four times over, because he did such a thing and had no pity."[6]

Sheep are popular pets, too, as can be seen by this photo, which was taken in 1918.

"While it had long been accepted that humans harnessed horses prior to riding them, new

---

[6] II Samuel 12:1-6, NIV

archeological research in Eurasia now may push the date for the first horseback riding back to approximately 4,000 BC. Excavations from Dereivka in the Ukrainian steppes have unearthed horse teeth from this period, which show possible signs of bit wear. This would mean that man became mounted shortly after domestication – some 3,000 years prior to significant horseback riding in the "civilized" Near East."

"As these people had no written language, were nomadic, and utilized materials which have not survived, little more is known of their early riding efforts. It would be more than 3,000 years before their legacy, the mounted Sythian cavalry, would make their presence felt in the 'civilized' world around 670 BC."

Thanks to the International Museum of the Horse, Lexington, Kentucky, for this background history of the horse.

According to Rev. J. G. Wood's book, *Story Of The Bible Animals*, in Bible days:

"The Arab lived with his horse, and found in it the docility and intelligence which we are accustomed to associate with the dog rather than the horse. It will follow him about and come at his call. It will stand for any length of time and await its rider without moving. Should he fall from its back, it will stop and stand patiently by him until he can remount; and there is a well-authenticated instance of an Arab horse whose master had been wounded in battle, taking him up by his clothes and carrying him away to a place of safety."

Wood, Rev. J. G. *Story Of The Bible Animals.*
Charles Foster Publishing Co., 1888.

One way in which we are able to learn about the history of animals as pets is from art and the gravestones of children. The following quotes from *Coming of Age in Ancient Greece: Images of childhood from the classical past* provide some information on the history of animals as pets. There are many photos of gravestones or steles and vases showing children with their beloved pets. A stele is a standing stone used in the ancient world primarily as a grave marker.

"The earliest gravestones showing a single child come from East Greece and the Aegean Islands. One of the most famous is the Parian "Dove Stele" of 450 BC. It shows a pensive young girl in a peplos who stands in a contrapposto pose in profile to the right with a pair of doves. One bird sits perched on her left hand, its body in a three-quarter pose, head turned nearly frontally, as birds are prone to do. The other she cuddles to her chest, leaning slightly forward to kiss its bill, as she displays affection for her pets. Birds are commonly shown with children on gravestones and their skeletal remains have also been found in children's graves."

Neils, Jenifer and Oakley, John H. *Coming Of Age In Ancient Greece, Images of Childhood from the Classical Past.* Yale University Press, 2003, Page 180.

On the cover of this book is a stele called the Gravestone of the Girl Melisto dated 340 BC.

> "This charming young girl of six to eight years old is happily engrossed with her playthings, her pleasure evident in the broad, happy smile upon her face. She stands in a three-quarter view to the right, with head nearly in profile, right leg drawn back. In her right hand she holds a bird toward which a Maltese dog with curled tail jumps, balancing itself on its hind legs. This is a common motif on children's gravestones."

> Neils, Jenifer and Oakley, John H. *Coming Of Age In Ancient Greece, Images of Childhood from the Classical Past.* Yale University Press, 2003, Pages 181 and 307.

Another example is:

> "A lekythos or vase showing a picture of a youth with his cat dated 490 B.C.E. Domestic cats are often depicted in Greek art. The cat on this vase has been thought to resemble most closely the Abyssinian shorthair, the Egyptian domestic cat that was imported into Athens. Greek children had many of the standard types of pets we have today, including cats, dogs, and birds, as well as oddities like the weasel."

> Neils, Jenifer and Oakley, John H. *Coming Of Age In Ancient Greece, Images of Childhood from the Classical Past.* Yale University Press, 2003, Page 281.

"Queen Alexandra (1844-1925) of England had a colony of doves and Australian birds at Sandringham. She never forgot the crumbs of bread, biscuit, and bits of sugar to feed them. The famous Cockatoo "Cockie" was for years a regular boarder in her majesty's dressing room. At Frogmore she had racing pigeons, turtles, and other animals."

The Brooklyn Public Library, Brooklyn Eagle newspaper article dated November 6, 1901, Brooklyn, New York.

Queen Alexandra is known to have had dogs and other animals, as well.

Most of the US Presidents have had pets. Abraham Lincoln (1809-65) had a dog named Jip, and other pets. George Washington (1732-99) had several dogs, cats, and a parrot.

Walt Disney (1901-66) had a dog named Carey, a poodle named Lady, and a pet mouse called Mortimer, who was the inspiration for Mickey Mouse.

Beatrix Potter, (1866-1943) the British children's book illustrator and writer had cats, dogs, rabbits, frogs, lizards, pigs, and hedgehogs.

Some pets are less typical than cats, dogs, birds, and horses. The Boston Globe had an article on December 16, 2004 about some unusual family pets. It states, "The chicken moves up in the pecking order of desirable family pets, and fresh eggs are just a bonus." Some people keep chickens as pets, while others may like goats or roosters. We've had prayer requests on our website for pet squirrels, pigeons, and even a skunk.

The love affair with our pets is probably stronger than ever today. The following story reflects this fact.

"A woman named Tracy threw herself into the frigid East River in January 2005 to rescue her precious dog, Cho. The desperate dog owner ran up and down a sheer wall that drops 10 feet into the river, screaming for the seemingly doomed dog, a 25-pound Shiba Inu, which was being pulled by a strong current. She finally dove into the water, and with the help of some onlookers, they both came out to safety."

The New York Post, January 2005.

Our Animal Companion's Love For Us

Recently a man suffering from cancer, and his cat, Penny, both died at the same time in New Hampshire.

"As 74-year-old Bernard Richards began to lose the battle with cancer, even his beloved 3-year-old cat, Penny, appeared to be distressed. The cat stopped eating, then drinking, almost on cue with her owner. Then Bernard died peacefully early one morning surrounded by his children, wife, and Penny."

"Remarkably, Penny died only inches away from him at the same time. The family noticed that Penny was depressed and having problems, but they were so preoccupied with Bernard that they hadn't had a chance to take her to a vet yet. Bernard and Penny were buried together in a New Hampshire Veterans Cemetery."

The Telegraph, Front Page, August 13, 2005,
Nashua, New Hampshire.

"A farmer in Australia who suffered serious head injuries after being struck by a falling tree branch was rescued by a partially blind kangaroo who was hailed as a hero. Lulu the kangaroo banged on the door of the family's home in Morwell, Gippsland in southeast Australia after discovering the farmer lying unconscious in a field."

"According to Rural Ambulance Victoria paramedic, Eddie, the man had been checking his property for damage following a severe storm when he was struck by the branch. Wright said that if Len's family had not found him so quickly, he might have died. 'The kangaroo alerted them to where he was and went and sat down next to him, and that's how they found him,' he said."

"Len was taken to an Austin hospital. Len's daughter Celeste said, 'Lulu and Dad are very close and she follows him around, but we all just love her so much.' About ten years ago, the family found Lulu in the pouch of her mother who had been killed by a car. The authorities allowed them to care for Lulu and adopt her, because she is missing one eye."

Portsmouth Herald, April 29, 2004, Portsmouth, New Hampshire.

"A bull that pined for its owner had to be led away from his grave after a vigil lasting a number of days. Barnaby the bull left his field in the German town of Roedental, and found his way to the cemetery where his owner was buried. The eccentric farmer is said to have treated his animals like pets, allowing several to have the run of his house. They said that it seemed incredible that a bull could find the exact spot where his master was buried."

Ananova News, www.anaova.com.

"Tragically, a woman named Shirley, in Massachusetts was murdered. She had a pet goat named Ricky. After Shirley died, Ricky withdrew, looked thin and weak. Ricky was mourning the loss of Shirley. Fortunately, a friend of Shirley's adopted Ricky, and he has become a favorite among the whole town. After a couple of months Ricky became happy and healthy again."

The Boston Globe, July 17, 2005, Boston, Massachusetts.

Gary from Columbus, Ohio, adopted his cat, Tommy, three years earlier to help lower his blood pressure. Gary tried to train his cat to call 911, and he wasn't sure if his training worked. Then one day Gary fell out of his wheelchair, and couldn't get up because of pain from osteoporosis and ministrokes that disrupt his balance. Tommy dialed 911 and called for help. The cat was lying by a telephone on the living room floor when the officer went in. Tommy saved Gary's life!

Dayton Daily News, Dayton, Ohio, December 31, 2005.

Michael from California knew he had a loyal friend in his dog, Honey, but he became a life savor for Michael. The cocker spaniel was with Michael when he backed out a little too far from his driveway, sending his SUV plunging 40 feet into a remote ravine. The vehicle landed on its roof, pinning Michael inside.

After several hours, Honey was able to escape when Michael managed to roll down the window, and told the dog to go for help. She ran half a mile to their neighbor's house, Robin. "She was bringing me here," Robin said, "She was directing me."

By the time rescuers reached the scene, Michael had been hanging upside down for more than six hours – and his pulse was weakening. Honey saved his life just in time. Ironically, Michael had recently saved hers when he adopted her from a shelter two weeks earlier. By giving Honey a new home, Michael gave himself a new lease on life!

ABC News Internet Ventures, November 2, 2005.

In upstate New York Edward's dog remained asleep, but his cat woke him up, alerting him to a fire in the bedroom. He quickly called the fire department, and was treated for smoke inhalation. Edward's cat saved all of their lives, and thank God, he and his pets were not hurt.

Kirotv.com, February 28, 2007.

An alert tabby saved an Australian family from a house fire by clawing at his owner's face. Timmy the tabby sprang into action by waking his owner when a mattress caught fire as the family slept early in the morning in Cairns in Australia's tropical north. The fire department said "The cat was probably the best smoke alarm system. He was clawing at the owner's face and got him up and out of bed."

Reuters, January 2, 2007.

Jesus And The Animals

It's very interesting that Jesus seemed to be around animals often, and He frequently used animals in His parables. It would appear that Jesus had animals on His mind. Let's take a look at some of these examples.

Jesus was born in a manger, which is a feeding trough for livestock, and was surrounded by animals. Isn't it interesting that of all the places that Jesus could have potentially been born, that it was in a stable with the animals?

"So they hurried off and found Mary and Joseph, and the baby, who was lying in the manger."[7]

The Holy Spirit descended on Jesus in the form of a dove when John was baptizing Him. It's interesting that the third person of the Godhead, The Holy Spirit, appeared in animal form.

"At that time Jesus came from Nazareth in Galilee and was baptized by John in the Jordan. As Jesus was coming up out of the water, He saw Heaven being torn open and the Spirit descending on Him like a dove.

---

[7] Luke 2:16, KJV

And a voice came from Heaven: 'You are My Son, whom I love; with You I am well pleased.'"[8]

Right after He was baptized, the Holy Spirit led Him out into the desert where He fasted for 40 days. The wild animals and the angels were the only ones to surround him.

"At once the Spirit sent Him out into the desert, and He was in the desert forty days, being tempted by Satan. He was with the wild animals, and angels attended Him."[9]

His conversation frequently involved animals. He said to the disciples, "I will make you fishers of men."[10] In fact, most of the disciples were fishermen.

Jesus taught that it is easier for a camel to go through the eye of a needle than for a rich man to enter the Kingdom of God.[11]

Jesus told Peter to go down to the sea and throw in his hook and the first fish he catches will have a shekel in it. He was told to go and pay both their taxes.[12] Even Jesus had to pay taxes!

In the Bible, Jesus is called the Lamb of God.[13]

He's called the Good Shepherd. "I am the Good Shepherd; I know My sheep and My sheep know Me."'[14]

Jesus is referred to as The Lion of Judah.

"Then one of the elders said to me, "Do not weep! See, the Lion of the tribe of Judah, the Root of David, has

---

[8] Mark 1:9-11, KJV
[9] Mark 1:12-13, KJV
[10] Matthew 4:18-22, KJV
[11] Matthew 19:23-24, KJV
[12] Matthew 17:27, KJV
[13] Revelation Chapter 5
[14] John 10:14, KJV

triumphed. He is able to open the scroll and its seven seals."[15]

Another example of Jesus using animals in His conversation is when He referred to hens and chicks.

"O Jerusalem, Jerusalem, you who kill the prophets and stone those sent to you, how often I have longed to gather your children together, as a hen gathers her chicks under her wings, but you were not willing.[16]

He talks about the Sheep and the Goats in these next verses.

---

[15] Revelation 5:5, KJV
[16] Matthew 23:37, KJV

"When the Son of Man comes in His glory, and all the angels with Him, He will sit on His throne in Heavenly glory. All the nations will be gathered before Him, and He will separate the people one from another as a shepherd separates the sheep from the goats. He will put the sheep on His right and the goats on His left."

"Then the King will say to those on His right, 'Come, you who are blessed by My Father; take your inheritance, the kingdom prepared for you since the creation of the world. For I was hungry and you gave Me something to eat, I was thirsty and you gave Me something to drink, I was a stranger and you invited Me in, I needed clothes and you clothed Me, I was sick and you looked after Me, I was in prison and you came to visit Me.'"

"Then the righteous will answer Him, 'Lord, when did we see You hungry and feed You, or thirsty and give You something to drink? When did we see You a stranger and invite You in, or needing clothes and clothe You? When did we see You sick or in prison and go to visit You?'"

"The King will reply, 'I tell you the truth, whatever you did for one of the least of these brothers of Mine, you did for Me.'"[17]

Just before Jesus went to the cross, the Bible says that He told the disciples to get a donkey and bring it to Him. He rode the donkey into Jerusalem to go to the cross.[18]

The Bible says that when Jesus returns He will ride a white horse. He could ride in any type of vehicle He wished or simply fly down, but He has chosen to ride a white horse! Jesus must love animals!

---

[17] Matthew 25:31-40, KJV
[18] Luke Chapter 19

"I saw Heaven standing open and there before me was a white horse, whose rider is called Faithful and True. With justice He judges and makes war."[19]

Jesus made the once-and-for-all sacrifice for us by dying on the cross. It also eliminated the necessity for animals to ever be sacrificed again!

Did you ever notice that when a person really loves someone, they talk about them all the time? That's because they are thinking about them so much. Jesus obviously loves the animals very much, because He had them on His mind so often!

In reviewing this chapter, we can see by all this information that as long as we have had historical records, we see proof that there has been a love and bond between people and their pets.

Susie Meskell and her dog, Bambie.
Bambie lives in Heaven now!

---

[19] Revelation 19:11, KJV

Chapter 3

Encouraging And Miraculous Stories

Pete's In Heaven!

Pete Shanahan

Our Life With Pete

Growing up, our family didn't have any pets, so I didn't give much thought to having a companion animal. I suppose if you never had one, you don't know what you're missing. My husband, Jack, always had cats in his family growing up. When Jack and I were first married, we lived on the second floor in a condominium. Little did we know who was living on the first floor – it was Pete!

One day we heard a cat meowing in the hallway outside our door. Jack dashed to the door and let the cat in. It really didn't matter much to me if he let him in or not at that time. Pete kept visiting us, each time meowing outside the door for admittance. One day I was writing at the kitchen table when

Pete came in. He got up on the chair beside me, and I looked into the most beautiful green eyes I had ever seen! On other occasions he would walk around, and rub up against my legs as I did the dishes at the sink. Little by little this short fluffy bundle of love stole my heart!

Then it happened. I started looking for him – I was hooked! We started feeding Pete on a regular basis, and he would stay for long periods of time.

One night he didn't leave, sleeping on a rocking chair in the living room all night. Finally, I discovered that he belonged to Judy on the first floor. I said to her, "your cat has been coming by to visit me, and he stayed overnight a couple of times. I hope you weren't worried about him." She said, "no, if he bothers you, just throw him out." Judy said that she was getting married in a couple of months, and she didn't know what she was going to do with Pete, because her fiancé had a dog that couldn't tolerate other animals. That was the day that I decided I would definitely adopt him. We named him Pete, a name I always liked. It has a nice sound – Pete Shanahan! Judy also told me that he was 8 years old.

Jack was going to night school and was busy with that most of his spare time, so Pete and I kept each other company. Pete would get up with us in the morning and have breakfast – he was always very vocal about being fed promptly! He would sleep on our bed, usually laying on my legs all night, sit on my lap in the evening, nap in my arms, and play toy and flashlight games with Jack.

He'd let you put a little rubber duck on his head, and allow us to be amused by it – Pete was a good sport. He was very cooperative the year I put a Santa hat on his head, and asked him to pose for our Christmas cards. He loved to sit under the Christmas tree. When I would bring the tree into the house and lay it against the wall before setting it up, Pete would sit under it – ready to start celebrating right away. He loved to open his toys at Christmas, and exchange gifts and cards with his Grandma and Auntie every year.

The White Angel Cat

Fourteen wonderful years had passed. It was a couple of weeks before Pete passed away that he was sitting on the bay window in the dining room. I went over to see him, and there I saw a beautiful, pure white cat outside directly in front of the window where he sat. The white cat was staring up at Pete. I called Jack, to come over to see this white cat that seemed to be in a trance as she gazed up at Pete. Jack came over to take a look, and within a couple of minutes she vanished from sight.

I immediately ran outside to leave her some food in case she came back, but all the while I had an uneasy feeling inside me that this was no ordinary cat. There are very few outdoor cats in our neighborhood; we never saw this white cat before, and we've never seen her since. I couldn't get it out of my mind that the beautiful feline was an angel, or an angel in the appearance of a cat, ready to take Pete to Heaven. I asked Jack if we could pray for Pete a little later that night and we did.

Within a couple of weeks Pete did pass away on December 15, 2001. I believe that this angel cat was sent by God to gently let us know that Pete was going home soon.

The Book Proving That All Animals Go To Heaven

Pete lived to be close to 22 years old, which is a long lifespan for a cat, but not long enough when you love someone. He enjoyed a very loving life with us, and was really only sick the last year of his life. Even though it pains us deeply that he is gone, we know he's with the Lord in Heaven waiting for us to join him someday.

The great bond between Pete and I was my inspiration to research the Bible to see what God had to say about the afterlife of animals. I found many Scriptures in my research, and I felt the need to document it in an organized way. Once I began to type everything in a file, I said to Jack, "I think this is a book!" I was delighted with my findings that proved Scripturally that all the animals go to Heaven. I titled the book; *"There Is Eternal Life For Animals."*

A Miracle Exactly One Year Later

Photo of The Cross Of Snow

On December 15, 2002, it was exactly one year since Pete passed away. I was feeling very depressed, and just moping around the house. I looked out the window and noticed that it was snowing. Later I looked out the back window at the place where Pete was buried, right under the huge rock. I had to look twice, because there was a snow shaped cross on the huge rock right over Pete's grave! Why isn't there any snow on the rest of the rock? There's snow everywhere else, on the trees, on the grass, everywhere. But on the rock it was only in the shape of a cross. See photo above.

After the snow was gone I went to see what the rock looked like, and I noticed that there was a branch, which formed the vertical part of the cross, horizontally it looks like an indent in the rock. We have photos of the rock fully covered with snow, and others with the snow melting, and we have a photo of the rock with the "Cross of Snow." The branch remained there throughout the winter, but we didn't see the Cross of Snow again – **only on the one-year anniversary of Pete's passing.** I know it's a sign from God that Pete is alive and well in Heaven!

He gave us this sign to comfort us, and reaffirm our beliefs that Pete is in Heaven. I believe that God wants us to share this story with all those who are feeling the pain at the loss of their animal companions. It's true that God preserves people and animals.[20]

I often wonder what it's like in Heaven, and what everybody is doing. Sometimes I imagine Pete's playing with the other animals, perhaps riding on a big elephant! I'm sure he's spending time with my Dad, who passed away a couple of months before him. He and his Uncle Johnny, my brother who passed away at only three years old, are no doubt enjoying each other's company.

Now whenever I feel sad about my boy being gone, I stop and think – now I have something to look forward to. I'm going home to Pete someday, and we're going to live forever in Heaven! Then after 10,000 years go by, I'm going to turn to Pete and say, "well son, what do you want to do today?"

---

[20]Psalm 36:6

One Hundred Year Old Near-Death Experience

I would like to share more quotes from a book called *Intra Muros,* which is Greek for "within the walls." It was written by Rebecca Ruter Springer (1832-1904) in 1898, David C. Cook Publishing Company. Rebecca was a very devout Christian, the daughter of Rev. Calvin W. Ruter, a Methodist Episcopal minister. Rebecca married William McKendree Springer, a judge and a member of congress for many years.

Over one hundred years old, *Intra Muros* is a classic book in the Christian tradition. While on her deathbed, Rebecca experienced a vision. After several days she recovered, and returned from her vision in Heaven. As she did recover from her illness, she felt that this vision was given as an example of what Heavenly life is like. The author states, "I may be able to partly tear the veil from the death we so dread, and show it to be only an open door into a new and beautiful phase of the life we now live." While she was in Heaven her brother-in-law said, "If only we could realize while we are yet mortals, that day by day we are building for eternity, how different our lives in many ways would be!"

Rebecca Sees Her Pet Dog, Sport

"Not far from our home we saw a group of children playing upon the grass, and in their midst was a beautiful great dog, over which they were rolling and tumbling with the greatest freedom. As we approached he broke away from them and came bounding to meet us, and crouched and fawned at my feet with every gesture of glad welcome."

"Do you not know him, auntie? Mae asked brightly. It is dear old Sport! I cried, stooping and placing my arms about his neck, and resting my head on his silken hair. Dear old fellow! How happy I am to have you here!"

"He responded to my caresses with every expression of delight, and Mae laughed aloud at our mutual joy."

"I have often wondered if I should not some day find him here. He surely deserves a happy life for his faithfulness and devotion in the other life. His intelligence and his fidelity were far above those of many human beings whom we count immortal."

"Did he not sacrifice his life for little Will? Yes; he attempted to cross the track in front of an approaching train, because he saw it would pass between him and his little master, and feared he was in danger. It cost his life. He always placed himself between any of us and threatened danger, but Will he seemed to consider his special charge."

"He was a gallant fellow – he deserves immortality. Dear, dear old Sport, you shall never leave me again! I said, caressing him fondly."

"At this he sprang to his feet, barking joyously, and galloped and frolicked before us the rest of the way home, then lay down upon the doorstep, with an upward glance and a wag of his bushy tail, as though to say, "See how I take you at your word!""

Springer, Rebecca Ruter. *Intra Muros*. David C. Cook Publishing Company, 1898.

A Child Reunited With Her Kitten

"I remember once seeing a beautiful little girl enter Heaven, the very first to come of a large and affectionate family. I afterward learned that the sorrowful cry of her mother was, 'Oh, if only we had someone there to meet her, to care for her!' She came, lovingly nestled in the Master's own arms, and a little later, as He sat, still caressing and talking to her, a remarkably fine Angora kitten, of which the child had been very fond, and which had sickened and died some weeks before, to her great sorrow, came running across the grass and sprang directly into her arms, where it lay contentedly."

"Such a glad cry as she recognized her little favorite, such a hugging and kissing as that kitten received, made joy even in Heaven! Who but our loving Father would have thought of such comfort for a little child?"

Springer, Rebecca Ruter. *Intra Muros*. David C. Cook Publishing Company, 1898.

The Salvation Army's Founder, General William Booth's Vision Of Heaven

We're all familiar with the Christian organization, The Salvation Army, and the wonderful work that it does. For almost 100 years The Salvation Army's trained employees and volunteers have served at disasters, which place a community at risk or destroy family security and well-being.

Counseling survivors, consoling the injured and distressed, comforting the bereaved, conducting funeral and memorial services, chaplaincy services to staff and volunteers. Where needed, mobile feeding units serve hot meals to survivors and relief personnel. Shelters may be established and maintained in Salvation Army facilities or other sites.

Programs include childcare, to allow adult family members to salvage personal effects, apply for long-term assistance, schedule reconstruction, and undertake other necessary tasks.

General William Booth (1878-1912) was the Founder of the Salvation Army, one of the most respected organizations in the world. General Booth had several visions of Heaven. In his rare antiquarian and out-of-print book called *Visions* dated 1906, General Booth records the following vision that he had:

> "The blue skies, the towering mountains, the green valleys, the shady groves, the luxuriant vineyards, the charming flowers, the flowing rivers – were all exquisitely beautiful beyond the power of language to describe."

> "Then in, about, and indeed everywhere, were the loveliest birds and the most graceful of animals. I was enraptured with the scene. I was certainly a little surprised to find these living creatures here, having been always rather skeptical as to the resurrection of the animal world. There, however, they certainly were."

Booth, General William. *Visions.* London: The Salvation Army Printing Works, 1906.

Sparkey's Story

"A few years ago a friend of ours, a really wonderful lady named Lou, was diagnosed with terminal breast cancer. At the time of this sad diagnosis, it was too late for the doctors to do much to help Lou. A mutual friend of ours, named Jan, was Lou's very best friend in the whole world. Jan was also a registered nurse, and had experienced being with many people at the end of life."

"Over the years, and on many occasions, Jan and I would have "discussions" about whether or not animals would be waiting for us when we die. I always contended that they would be, because the Bible says that there are white horses at the right hand of God, so it always seemed to me that if there were white horses, there would be other animals waiting for us as well. Jan's firm stance was that animals did not have souls, therefore they could not go to Heaven, and they would not be there waiting to greet us. (Her strict religious upbringing was coming through.)"

"As Lou became more and more ill, and grew even closer to death, Jan stayed with her day and night. Lou finally sank into a deep coma and stayed there for three solid weeks. When she died, Jan was there with her, by her side."

"Jan called me the next morning to tell me that Lou had passed away the night before. But Jan didn't tell me the rest of the story for several weeks to come."

"You see, it seems that on the night that Lou died she awoke suddenly from her coma. Her eyes opened and she said one single, solitary word. Lou exclaimed in a quiet, weakened whisper, "SPARKY!" And then just as suddenly as she had awakened, she died."

"None of Lou's family knew who "Sparky" was. Not her husband of 45 years, not her grown children, not Jan, no one."

"A couple of weeks later, Jan got a call from Lou's family, asking her to please come to their home as soon as possible. It seemed they had something of great importance to show to her. When Jan arrived, Lou's family greeted her with a smile, and then put something in Jan's hand."

"It was an old black and white picture of a little girl, and a German Shepherd. On the back it was hand written in faded ink . . .'**Lou, Age 10, and Sparky!'**"

This story is used with permission by
Robin Pressnall.
Small Paws Rescue
www.smallpawsrescue.org

A Dying Boy Sees His Deceased Dog

"A few months ago, our church was affected by the illness and then death of a little boy with a terminal illness. His parents posted emails to church members to let us know how his day was going and to keep in touch with everyone, since they could not attend church due to his need for constant care. The mother posted a very touching email just a few days before her son passed. In this email, she told us that she heard her son talking to someone in his room."

"When she entered the room, no one was there. However, when she questioned her son as to whom he was talking to, he responded by telling her the 'little girls came here to visit.' His mother knew in her heart that the angels had come to prepare her son for Heaven."

"But then later that day, her son yelled out to her, 'Mom, come here!!' His mother immediately ran into his room, not knowing what to expect. Then, her sweet innocent son told her, 'Mom, Rusty came back. He's here!' Rusty was their little dog that they had to sadly put to sleep just a few months earlier due to illness.

Right then and there, all of my concerns were put to rest – indeed, animals do go to Heaven. I believe that the Lord not only sent the "little angel girls" to visit this sweet child, but also sent his beloved little dog, Rusty, to help him prepare the way to Heaven."

"A few days later, this sweet boy entered into Heaven's Gates. I have no doubt that his little furry friend, Rusty, was there to greet him!!"

This story is used with permission by Cheryl Johnson.

Other People Who Have Seen Pets And Animals In Heaven During NDEs and OBEs

Many Christians are uncomfortable about near-death (NDE) and out-of-body (OBE) experiences; however, in the Bible you'll find that the Apostle Paul, in fact, had a near-death experience or an out-of-body experience, and he saw things that he was not permitted to tell anyone about. He said whether he was in the body or out of the body, he didn't know.[21]

Also, the Disciple John, had a vision on the Isle of Patmos, which seems likely that it was an out-of-body experience.[22] Another out-of-body experience recorded in the Bible was Stephen who was stoned to death. When they were about to kill him, he looked up to Heaven and said, "I see Jesus standing on the right hand of God."[23]

In 1849 Marietta Davis had visions of Heaven when she was ill, and fell into a trance or a sleep. In the book *Scenes Beyond The Grave*, which was edited by Gordon Lindsay, the founder

---

[21] 2 Corinthians 12:2
[22] Revelation Chapter 1
[23] Acts 7:54-60

of Christ For The Nations, she tells of birds of all colors in Heaven. Here is a quote from that book:

> "There appeared stately edifices and streets lined with trees whose foliage cast a lovely shade; on whose branches birds of all colors appeared; and although all were singing with different notes, all mingled in one full and perfect harmony. Many corresponded to those on earth, and yet were as superior to them as the Paradise itself was superior to the mortal world."

> Davis, Marietta. *Scenes Beyond The Grave* Edited by Gordon Lindsay. Christ For The Nations, 1990.

H. A. Baker wrote a very interesting book called, *Visions Beyond The Veil: God's Revelation to Children of Heaven and Hell.*. H. A. Baker and his wife, Josephine, served as missionaries from the United States to Tibet during the period of 1911-1919. The Bakers became aware of teenage beggar boys starving and dying in the streets, and decided to open the Adullam Home, an orphanage where these young men received food, clean clothes, and learned about Jesus.

There were forty boys in Adullam Home when a great miracle took place; the Holy Spirit was poured out strongly upon these teenage boys. Falling under the power of God, they saw into the next world and visited Heaven. Their visits were so real that the children thought their souls had left their bodies to go to Heaven and returned. H. A. Baker recounted their visions and the glories they saw. Here are some quotes from that book:

> "The children held the little pets in their arms and passed them from one to another. Or perhaps they found the lion peacefully lying beneath a tree. In that case they climbed on his back, ran their fingers through

his shaggy mane, brushed his face, and put their hands in his mouth."

"If they so desired they curled down beside him to enjoy together the love of their common Maker. Why not? Somewhere "the wolf also shall dwell with the lamb and the leopard shall lie down with the kid; and the calf and the young lion and the fatling together; and a little child shall lead them. Their young ones shall lie down together."[24]

"Little children rode the small deer, while older children rode the larger deer or the friendly elephant. All was perfect love. All was great harmony. Such shouts of joy! Such happy childish laughter! Who but our Father in Heaven ever thought of or planned such a Paradise?"

> Baker, H. A. *Visions Beyond The Veil: God's Revelation to Children of Heaven and Hell.* Gabriel Resources, 2002.

In an Anglican Church newsletter, I found the testimony of a vision as follows:

"I had hesitated to send my 'vision' of an earlier pet cat – but with the two wonderful stories of the apparent afterlife of pets, I'd like to add my own, which has been for over 20 years confirmation for me of so many religious promises and beliefs."

"The cat, Samantha, which had started our long procession of adopted and rescued cats and dogs, was in her final illness. In the wee small hours she became congested and restless – accepting petting, but not wanting to be held. She kept obviously trying to move to something beyond her, having a hard time staying on

---

[24] Isaiah 11:6-8

her feet, but getting up and moving forward, meowing faintly. Finally, she gave an almost joyous loud cry, and sank to her feet, breathing her last."

"Almost immediately I heard a loud rushing sound, and saw a huge white light, which became almost like a large movie screen. There was a scene of a small stream, across from which was a brilliant landscape of green foliage and gorgeous flowers. Suddenly, our Samantha was seen carefully stepping on stones crossing the stream. She reached the other side, turned and looked back at me, and then bounded up the hill on the other side, like a kitten, looking back once more before continuing on. There was a sudden popping sound, and the vision disappeared, and I was left with Samantha's lifeless form beside me – but with a new and relaxed young appearance on her face."

"God uses animals to reach us – a little sparrow does not fall unnoticed. Neither do dogs or cats – or humans."

Near-Death Experiences (NDE) of Children

Children don't read books on near-death experiences; they don't watch TV specials on them either. They don't read complicated parts of the Bible that describe Heaven, such as in the book of Revelation. Therefore, I believe that what they say is true. Who tells them about tunnels and bright lights? Here are a couple of near-death experiences of children who have seen their pets in Heaven.

"Pat was interviewed at age 9 concerning his near drowning at age 7. Medical records documented that he lost spontaneous heartbeat and respirations, and cardiac resuscitation was required after he fell off a bridge into the water while fishing. He stated he floated out of his body and 'was up in the clouds. I was a little bit scared. I looked down and saw my body on a stretcher and saw Jim (a medic) with his head in his hands. Then I went into this tunnel. I wanted to go, but Abbie and Andy licked me and nagged me to go back.' Abbie and Andy were his former dog and cat who had died. He further stated that time did not exist while in the tunnel. An amateur photographer present at the scene of the rescue photographed a picture of the medic, Jim, sitting with his head in his hands. Reportedly, Pat had not seen or heard of the picture before his description of his NDE."

"Near Death Experiences and Death-Related Visions in Children: Implications for the Clinician," Melvin L. Morse, MD.

"My first near-death experience occurred when I was 13 years old, in September of 1972. It happened during open-heart surgery that I had to correct a heart condition I had had almost from the time of my birth. I was 2 weeks old when the condition was discovered. For 12 years I couldn't run and play like other kids. Occasionally, I would turn blue. Then I got real sick. The two weeks before surgery I was so scared. I would have my large, black Great Dane, Harvey, climb into bed with me. I would hold him tight and cry into his coat because I didn't want to die."

"The last thing I remember in surgery was a male voice saying in a very matter-of-fact way, 'Uh-oh, we have a problem here.' The next thing I knew I was floating up around the ceiling looking down on my body. My chest was open wide and I could see my internal organs. I remember thinking how odd it was that my organs were pearl gray and looked almost beautiful."

"Suddenly, I had to move on, so I floated into the waiting room where my parents were. There I saw my father with his head buried in my mother's lap. He was kneeling at her feet, his arms wrapped around her waist, and he was sobbing like nothing I had ever seen before. His whole body shook with the force of his sobs. My mother was stroking his head, whispering to him. This scene shocked me. Yet I felt distanced from the whole scene, because I knew they would be fine no matter what happened. Once I realized this, I felt myself being pulled into a tunnel that was horizontal."

"From the white light came two dogs of mine that had died. One was a collie named Mimi, who had died three years previously from an infection, and the other was a boxer named Sam who had died two years previously from being hit by a car. The dogs came running toward me, and jumped on me, and kissed my face with their tongues. Their tongues weren't wet, and I felt no weight when they jumped on me. The dogs seemed to glow from a light that was inside them. I remember thinking, 'Thank you, God, for letting my dogs be alive.' I hugged my dogs as tight as I could."

"I then called my dogs and together we started walking toward the light. All the colors were in the light and it was warm, a living thing, and there were people as far as the eye could see, and they were glowing with a light that seemed to come from within them – just like my dogs. In the distance I could see fields, hills, and a sky. The light spoke, and it said, 'Lynn, it is not time for you yet. Go back, child.'"

"I know this is going to sound silly, but I asked the light, 'If I go, can I come back, and will my dogs still be here waiting for me?' The light said yes, and then told me there were people who wanted to see me before I left. From out of the light came my maternal grandparents. I ran to them and embraced them. "

Atwater, P.M.H., Lh. D. *Children Of The New Millennium*. Three Rivers Press, 1999.

"Children are much more likely than adults to see former pets in a near-death experience. This is probably because they have lived much shorter lives, and have had fewer experiences. Their families and their pets are a very important part of their lives. In a survey of 300 children ages 3 to 13, researchers found that children considered that pets provide children a source of learning, happiness, comfort, and unconditional love."

Kidd and Kidd, 1985 *Psychological Reports 57*: 15-31.

Other Animals Seen In Heaven

Dr. Richard Sigmund is a minister from the Cleft of the Rock Ministries in Missouri. He wrote a book about his near-death experience in 1974. Apparently, Sigmund had been dead for over eight hours. He states in his book, *A Place Called Heaven,* that he saw children riding horses, and the horses had the power of speech and thought.

> "I saw them actually riding on some horses I saw in Heaven. The horses loved it and they loved the children. The horses had the power of speech, the power of thought – it was a wonderful experience – they could talk. And there were other creatures in Heaven."

> Sigmund, Richard. *A Place Called Heaven.*
> Lightfall Publishing, 2004, Page 36.

> "It was a mystery to me how the animals communicated. There were birds singing 'Amazing Grace.' And I knew every language, along with a Heavenly language, and could speak to anyone with perfect understanding."

> Sigmund, Richard. *A Place Called Heaven.*
> Lightfall Publishing, 2004, Page 92.

"Heaven has animals. Revelation tells us the Lord returns riding a white horse. I was taken to an area where there were horse-like creatures. They were supernatural. Some of them had wings. Some had other supernatural abilities that we don't have. They could walk on the air if they need to. I saw chariots. Tens of thousands of chariots and beautiful horses to pull them. The horses were white, all white. Every horse I saw was white. They had red hoofs: fiery, crimson, red hoofs. And huge nostrils. They were about 10 to 15 times the biggest horses I have ever seen and were all muscle – no fat."

"There were other supernatural animals. I saw a beast that had the body of a giant bull, the neck of a camel, and the head of a horse. And I saw an angel sitting on it. I was not told its purpose."

> Sigmund, Richard. *A Place Called Heaven.* Lightfall Publishing, 2004, Pages 110-111.

Roberts Liardon is a minister who is the founder and senior pastor of Embassy Christian Center and Spirit Life Bible College in Laguna Hills, CA. Even as a child, Liardon was devoted to God. He had an out-of-body experience, and went to Heaven when he was 8 years old while reading his Bible on his bed. He tells the story about this experience in his book, *We Saw Heaven*.

"Jesus and I continued walking, and as we crossed some hills, I noticed other things. I saw all kinds of animals, every kind you could think of, from A to Z. While I was in Heaven, I saw a dog, a baby goat, and a lion of great strength. There were birds singing in the trees, all sizes of birds, and they seemed to be singing the same song. I found that I could understand what they were singing – there was no 'communication gap.' When they stopped singing, it seemed as if they began to talk among themselves."

"There were other animals I saw at a distance, but I could not identify them. They neither ran from people nor tried to attack them, however. All were calm and peaceful, because fear cannot be found in Heaven. God's presence is so strong that there is no confusion, doubt, sickness or worry there."

> Liardon, Roberts. *We Saw Heaven.* Insight Publishing Group, 2000, Page 39.

Rev. Jesse Duplantis is an evangelist who has a weekly television program on the Trinity Broadcasting Network and other stations. He also speaks at churches, Bible colleges, and seminars. Duplantis had an out-of-body vision of Heaven. In his book, *Heaven: Close Encounters of the God Kind,* he states:

> "I saw horses, dogs, and large cats like lions in Heaven."

> Duplantis, Jesse. *Heaven: Close Encounters Of The God Kind.* Tulsa: Harrison House, 1996, Page 71.

The visions that we have shared in this chapter are yet another confirmation that the animals and people continue to live after they die. It is so encouraging to read these amazing testimonies of a future and eternal life for our beloved animal companions and us.

Chapter 4

You're Not Dead When You Die

"The report of my death was an exaggeration."
Mark Twain

In this chapter we will study what the Bible says about life after death. As you read this chapter you'll see that "You're Not Dead When You Die." The only part of our triune being that dies is our body.

After my cat, Pete, left it was extremely important to me to know that he was alive, well, happy, and in Heaven waiting for me. It's a tremendous comfort and hope to look forward to a reunion where we will never be separated again. To understand, believe, and have faith that your animal companion is still alive and well in Heaven, let's look at the subject of life after death.

The whole basis for believing in an afterlife originates from the Bible. The reason that people believe, and look forward to a new life in Heaven is because this is what the Bible teaches. If you have faith in God that you will live again after you die, then you can have faith in God that your pet continues to live once they leave you.

If you struggle with the belief that God has prepared a permanent home for us and that we will be resurrected, pray and ask the Lord to reveal this to you in your spirit.

It's times like these when we begin to think about what life is all about. We're suddenly snapped into the reality of the spiritual world. Heaven now becomes a very real place where our pets wait for us, and we develop a keen interest in what is taking place in that other world.

The Apostle Paul said,

> "If in this life only we have hope in Christ, we are of all men most miserable."[25]

What he meant was that if the life we live on earth is all there is, we would all be miserable and depressed. There would be nothing to look forward to. However, as it turns out, our lives on earth are actually the gateway to eternal life.

---

[25] I Corinthians 15:19, KJV

Understanding The Concept Of The Body, The Soul, And The Spirit

When my father-in-law passed away recently, my two little nieces were at the wake, but they stayed in the adjoining room. My niece, Jenny, was about 6 years old, and she was asking me questions about my father-in-law, such as, "where is he." I tried to explain that the real person inside of him was in Heaven, but she said, "I don't get it." I further tried to explain that even though his body was here, his spirit had gone up to Heaven to be with Jesus, and she said, "I still don't get it." I think we've all felt this way at one time or another.

When God created us He started with dust. God created the animals[26] and man,[27] and the Bible states that we will return to the dust.[28]

> "And out of the ground the Lord God formed every beast of the field, and every fowl of the air; and brought them unto Adam to see what he would call them: and whatsoever Adam called every living creature, that was the name thereof."[29]

It says that when animals die, their bodies return to the dust,[30] and it says that both people and animals return to the dust.[31] These are references to our physical bodies only.

Immortality is better understood if we can get a grip on the fact that we are all triune beings, both people and animals. Our composition consists of a body, a soul, and a spirit. Comprehending this truth will help us to realize that our loved ones go to Heaven when they leave earth, and that they are still quite alive.

---

[26] Genesis 1:24
[27] Genesis 1:26, 2:7
[28] Genesis 3:19
[29] Genesis 2:19, KJV
[30] Psalm 104:29
[31] Ecclesiastes 3:20

The Apostle Paul states that we have a body, a soul, and a spirit in this verse:

> "I pray God your whole spirit and soul and body be preserved blameless unto the coming of our Lord Jesus Christ."[32]

Also, this verse.

> "For the Word of God is quick, and powerful, and sharper than any twoedged sword, piercing even to the dividing asunder of soul and spirit, and of the joints and marrow, and is a discerner of the thoughts and intents of the heart."[33]

In these next verses we see references to the soul and spirit.

> "And Mary said, My soul doth magnify the Lord. And my spirit hath rejoiced in God my Saviour."[34]

> "With my soul have I desired thee in the night; yea, with my spirit within me will I seek Thee early: for when Thy judgments are in the earth, the inhabitants of the world will learn righteousness."[35]

> "Therefore I will not refrain my mouth; I will speak in the anguish of my spirit; I will complain in the bitterness of my soul."[36]

> "And Hannah answered and said, No, my lord, I am a woman of a sorrowful spirit: I have drunk neither wine nor strong drink, but have poured out my soul before the Lord."[37]

Here's a reference to body and soul made by Jesus. When you're a born again Christian, only your body dies, and your soul and spirit live on in Heaven. Someday your body will be

---

[32] 1 Thessalonians 5:23, KJV
[33] Hebrews 4:12, KJV
[34] Luke 1:46-47, KJV
[35] Isaiah 26:9, KJV
[36] Job 7:11, KJV
[37] 1 Samuel 1:15, KJV

resurrected, and joined again with your soul and spirit for eternity. The point here is to reflect on where you will spend eternity.

> "Do not be afraid of those who kill the body but cannot kill the soul. Rather, be afraid of the one who can destroy both soul and body in hell."[38]

Notice that only the body dies, but the soul continues to live. Our earthly passing does not mark the end of existence, life, or consciousness. This reference to hell is intended toward people who are not right with God, and is not applicable toward the animals as they are sinless.[39]

This verse is concerning the body and spirit:

> "But if Christ is in you, your body is dead because of sin, yet your spirit is alive because of righteousness."[40]

We all know what the body is, but I believe it's understanding the difference between our soul and spirit that confuse us. The three elements of our being can be described by saying we are a spirit, and we posses a soul and body.

Body

Our outer shell.

Example: "We are confident, I say, and willing rather to be absent from the **body**, and to be present with the Lord."[41]

---

[38] Matthew 10:28, NIV
[39] Romans 8:18-23
[40] Romans 8:10, NIV
[41] 2 Corinthians 5:8, KJV

Soul

Our mind, intellect, emotion, willpower or the dominant self.

Examples: "Why art thou cast down, O my **soul**? And why art thou disquieted in me? Hope thou in God: for I shall yet praise Him for the help of His countenance."[42] Also, refer to the above-mentioned verses in Job 7:11 (bitterness of my **soul**) and 1 Samuel 1:15 (poured out my **soul**) which shows us that the **soul** has feelings and emotions.

Spirit

The spirit is the part that communicates with God.

Example: "God is a **Spirit**; and they that worship Him must worship Him in **spirit** and in truth."[43] Also, Isaiah 26:9 shown above, "with my **spirit** within me will I seek Thee early."

Relative to specific verses that tell us that animals also have souls and spirits, I would refer you to my previous work, *There Is Eternal Life For Animals*, Chapter 5, *Animals Have Souls and Spirits*. I will share a couple of the verses with you here.

"And God created great whales, and **every living creature** [*soul – nephesh*] that moveth, which the waters brought forth abundantly, after their kind, and every winged fowl after his kind: and God saw that it was good."[44]

---

[42] Psalm 42:5, KJV
[43] John 4:24, KJV
[44] Genesis 1:21, KJV

Also see Genesis 1:20, 24, 30, and Genesis 2:19. The next verse speaks about when all life was destroyed except Noah, his family, and the selected animals that were in the ark. This was because all the people were wicked except Noah and his family.

Unfortunately, all the animals that were not in the ark were affected by the sin of the people. It says that **"all in whose nostrils was the breath of the spirit of life"** were destroyed. This makes no distinction between man and the animals having **"the breath of the spirit of life."**

> "And all flesh died that moved on the earth: birds and cattle and beasts and every creeping thing that creeps on the earth, and every man. All in whose nostrils **was the breath of the spirit of life**, all that was on the dry land, died. So He destroyed all living things which were on the face of the ground: both man and cattle, creeping thing and bird of the air. They were destroyed from the earth. Only Noah and those who were with him in the ark remained alive. And the waters prevailed on the earth one hundred and fifty days."[45]

Having established the Scriptures revealing that all of God's creatures are triune beings, we can now proceed to learn about our future. First of all, God is not the God of any dead creatures, but He is the God of living creatures. Meaning that creatures never truly die – only their bodies die.

> **"For He is not a God of the dead, but of the living: for all live unto Him."**[46]

In Gordon Lindsay's book, *Death and the Hereafter,* he states:

> "The farmer sows a grain of wheat into the cold ground. It decays and dies. But lo, nature has reserved for it a miracle. For the dying seed, there springs forth new life! If the God of nature can do this with a little

---

[45] Genesis 7:21-24, NKJV
[46] Luke 20:38, KJV

insignificant seed, how much more surely will He do for man? Nature teaches that it is possible for an old body to be set aside for a superior body."

"There is the caterpillar, ugly, repulsive, crawling, representing life in its most rudimentary form. It lives, crawls, curls up, and then seemingly dies. To one who is uninformed, it would seem that life has vanished forever. But nature has a miracle awaiting it. Out of the ugly body of death comes forth a beautiful butterfly to wing its way about in its many iridescent colors. No longer bound to the earth, it takes its wings and flies up into the golden sunlight."

Lindsay, Gordon. *Death And The Hereafter.*
Christ For The Nations, 1978.

Resurrection From The Dead

It may sound incredible and even impossible for God to resurrect us from the dead, but we have Bible records of people coming back from the dead. Jesus Himself rose up from the grave after three days.[47] We've all heard the story of Jesus raising Lazarus from the dead. This is just a foretaste of how easy it's going to be for God to raise all of us from the dead someday.

Jesus Raises Lazarus From the Dead

"Jesus, once more deeply moved, came to the tomb. It was a cave with a stone laid across the entrance. 'Take away the stone,' he said. 'But, Lord,' said Martha, the sister of the dead man, 'by this time there is a bad odor, for he has been there four days.' Then Jesus said, 'Did I not tell you that if you believed, you would see the glory of God?' So they took away the stone. Then Jesus looked up and said, 'Father, I thank You that You have heard Me. I knew that you always hear me, but I

---

[47] Mark 16, Luke 24, and many more verses.

said this for the benefit of the people standing here, that they may believe that You sent Me.' When He had said this, Jesus called in a loud voice, 'Lazarus, come out!' The dead man came out, his hands and feet wrapped with strips of linen, and a cloth around his face. Jesus said to them, 'Take off the grave clothes and let him go.'"[48]

Others Raised From The Dead

The Bible shows us that there were other people that were brought back to life. There were two other times that we have a record of Jesus Himself raising people back to life. One was the daughter of a ruler of the synagogue named Jairus. He came to Jesus and told Him that his daughter, who was about twelve years old, had died. He asked Jesus to come home with him and heal her. When Jesus got there all the people were wailing and mourning over the girl. Jesus said to them, "stop wailing, she is not dead but asleep." They laughed at Him. But He took her by the hand and said, "my child, get up!" The Bible says her spirit returned, and at once she stood up.[49]

Another time Jesus raised a widow's son from the dead.

"Soon afterward, Jesus went to a town called Nain, and His disciples and a large crowd went along with Him. As He approached the town gate, a dead person was being carried out — the only son of his mother, and she was a widow. And a large crowd from the town was with her. When the Lord saw her, His heart went out to her and He said, 'Don't cry.'"

"Then He went up and touched the coffin, and those carrying it stood still. He said, 'Young man, I say to you, get up!' The dead man sat up and began to talk, and Jesus gave him back to his mother."[50]

---

[48] John 11:38-44, NIV
[49] Luke 8:41-56, NIV
[50] Luke 7:11-15, NIV

Was Jesus The Only One To Raise The Dead?

The resurrections were not limited to Jesus. Peter raised a Disciple named Dorcas from the dead.

> "In Joppa there was a disciple named Tabitha (which, when translated, is Dorcas), who was always doing good and helping the poor. About that time she became sick and died, and her body was washed and placed in an upstairs room. Lydda was near Joppa; so when the disciples heard that Peter was in Lydda, they sent two men to him and urged him, 'Please come at once!'"

> "Peter went with them, and when he arrived he was taken upstairs to the room. All the widows stood around him, crying and showing him the robes and other clothing that Dorcas had made while she was still with them."

> "Peter sent them all out of the room; then he got down on his knees and prayed. Turning toward the dead woman, he said, "Tabitha, get up." She opened her eyes, and seeing Peter she sat up. He took her by the hand and helped her to her feet. Then he called the believers and the widows and presented her to them alive."[51]

Paul raised a man named Eutychus from the dead, as well.

> "On the first day of the week we came together to break bread. Paul spoke to the people and, because he intended to leave the next day, kept on talking until midnight. There were many lamps in the upstairs room where we were meeting. Seated in a window was a young man named Eutychus, who was sinking into a deep sleep as Paul talked on and on. When he was sound asleep, he fell to the ground from the third story and was picked up dead. Paul went down, threw himself on the young man and put his arms around him.

---

[51] Acts 9:36-41, NIV

'Don't be alarmed,' he said. 'He's alive!' Then he went upstairs again and broke bread and ate. After talking until daylight, he left. The people took the young man home alive and were greatly comforted."[52]

In the Old Testament we have two other examples of the dead coming back to life. Elijah raised a widow's son[53] and Elisha raised a Shunammite's son from the dead.[54] Of course, these men were able to raise the dead through the power of the Lord, because they were very Godly men. God can do anything, and one day He will resurrect all of our bodies!

Absent From The Body, Present With The Lord

The Apostle Paul explains to us that once we are absent from the body, we are present with the Lord.

> "Therefore we are always confident, knowing that, whilst we are at home in the body, we are absent from the Lord: (For we walk by faith, not by sight:) We are confident, I say, and willing rather to be absent from the body, and to be present with the Lord."[55]

This verse is referring to Christians that have given their lives to the Lord, and have become born-again. If you haven't accepted the Lord, and want to be sure that you will go to Heaven and be reunited with your animal companion, as well as other loved ones, see the section in Chapter 7 entitled "Joining our animal companions in Heaven."

When Jesus was on the cross, the thief that was on a cross beside him said, "Jesus, remember me when You come into Your kingdom. Jesus answered him, I tell you the truth, today you will be with Me in Paradise."[56] Jesus told this man that as

---

[52] Acts 20:7-12, NIV
[53] 1 Kings 17:17-24
[54] 2 Kings 4:32-37
[55] 2 Corinthians 5:6-8
[56] Luke 23:42-43, NIV

soon as he died, (the same day) he would be in Paradise, which is another word used for Heaven. Even though this man had been a thief and done some wrong things in his life, he made a very good choice at the end of his life. He was repentant, and he believed that Jesus was the Son of God. Thus, he went to Heaven with Jesus.

In these next verses we see that the Apostle Paul was anticipating the time when he would leave the earth, and go to Heaven to be with Christ.

> "For to me, to live is Christ and to die is gain. If I am to go on living in the body, this will mean fruitful labor for me. Yet what shall I choose? I do not know! I am torn between the two: I desire to depart and be with Christ, which is better by far; but it is more necessary for you that I remain in the body."[57]

In other words, what Paul is saying is, do I hope it's my time to die, yes, I'd like to go to Heaven and be with Christ, because life is going to be so much better there. On the other hand, I know that the people here need me as a teacher of the Word of God, and to pray for them.

In Gordon Lindsay's book, *Life After Death*, he explains some Scriptures in Revelation regarding some specific people in Heaven who have died. There are people spoken of in the Bible that are martyred saints. They haven't yet been resurrected or given bodies, but they are resting until the powers of evil in the earth have finished their course.

At the time referred to, others are yet to be martyred for the cause of Christ. Now it is evident that these souls without bodies are very much conscious. Indeed they are not only conscious, but they are in eager anticipation of the hour when the judgments on earth shall be completed, and the great plan of God for His redeemed in the age to come shall begin to unfold. Here are the verses:

---

[57] Philippians 1:21-24, NIV

"When He opened the fifth seal, I saw under the altar the souls of those who had been slain because of the Word of God and the testimony they had maintained. They called out in a loud voice, 'How long, Sovereign Lord, holy and true, until You judge the inhabitants of the earth and avenge our blood?' Then each of them was given a white robe, and they were told to wait a little longer, until the number of their fellow servants and brothers who were to be killed as they had been was completed."[58]

Lindsay, Gordon. *Life After Death.* Christ For The Nations, 1988.

Heaven Is A Very Real Place

Apparently, the Apostle Paul had either an out-of-body or near-death experience that was wonderful, and he saw and heard amazing things in Heaven.

"I know a man in Christ who fourteen years ago was caught up to the third Heaven. Whether it was in the body or out of the body I do not know — God knows. And I know that this man — whether in the body or apart from the body I do not know, but God knows — was caught up to Paradise. He heard inexpressible things, things that man is not permitted to tell."[59]

The Disciple, Stephen, was stoned to death, and he had a vision of Heaven at the time of his death.

---

[58] Revelation 6:9-11, NIV
[59] 2 Corinthians 12:2-4, NIV

"But Stephen, full of the Holy Spirit, looked up to Heaven and saw the glory of God, and Jesus standing at the right hand of God. Look, he said, 'I see Heaven open and the Son of Man standing at the right hand of God.'"[60]

In some verses, written by the Apostle Paul, we see that Jesus was still quite alive after He died on the cross and was resurrected. It talks about Jesus being caught up into Heaven.

"In my former book, Theophilus, I wrote about all that Jesus began to do and to teach until the day He was taken up to Heaven, after giving instructions through the Holy Spirit to the apostles He had chosen. After His suffering, He showed Himself to these men and gave many convincing proofs that He was alive. He appeared to them over a period of forty days and spoke about the Kingdom of God."

"On one occasion, while He was eating with them, He gave them this command: 'Do not leave Jerusalem, but wait for the gift My Father promised, which you have heard Me speak about. For John baptized with water, but in a few days you will be baptized with the Holy Spirit.' So when they met together, they asked Him, Lord, are You at this time going to restore the Kingdom to Israel? He said to them: 'It is not for you to know the times or dates the Father has set by His own authority. But you will receive power when the Holy Spirit comes on you; and you will be My witnesses in Jerusalem, and in all Judea and Samaria, and to the ends of the earth.' After He said this, He was taken up before their very eyes, and a cloud hid Him from their sight."[61]

Many times I've looked up into the sky and the clouds, and I've wished I could see what was up in Heaven. I would love

---

[60] Acts 7:55-56, NIV
[61] Acts 1:1-11, NIV

to know what's going on up there, and what all our loved ones are doing. Perhaps you've done that as well.

Jesus told us that there are many mansions and places to live that are waiting for us in Heaven. Then we learn that Heaven is where our citizenship is, and where our real treasures are.

> "In my Father's house are many mansions: if it were not so, I would have told you. I go to prepare a place for you. And if I go and prepare a place for you, I will come again, and receive you unto Myself; that where I am, there ye may be also."[62]

"The Breakers" Newport, Rhode Island

Above is a picture of the Vanderbilt mansion "The Breakers" in Newport, Rhode Island. As elaborate as many mansions are here on earth, they cannot compare to what God has prepared for us in Heaven.

> "But our citizenship is in Heaven. And we eagerly await a Savior from there, the Lord Jesus Christ."[63]

> "But store up for yourselves treasures in Heaven, where moth and rust do not destroy, and where thieves do not break in and steal."[64]

---

[62] John 14:2, KJV
[63] Philippians 3:20, NIV
[64] Matthew 6:20, NIV

"Because we have heard of your faith in Christ Jesus and of the love you have for all the saints — the faith and love that spring from the hope that is stored up for you in Heaven and that you have already heard about in the Word of truth, the gospel that has come to you. All over the world this gospel is bearing fruit and growing, just as it has been doing among you since the day you heard it and understood God's grace in all its truth."[65]

"God created Heaven,[66] and He looks down at us from Heaven."[67]

Joe with his cat, Stanley

"So you must remain faithful to what you have been taught from the beginning. If you do, you will continue to live in fellowship with the Son and with the Father.

---

[65] Colossians 1:4-6, NIV
[66] Genesis 1:1
[67] Deuteronomy 26:15, Psalm 123:1

And in this fellowship we enjoy the eternal life He promised us."[68]

For more information on what Heaven is like, you can read Revelation chapters 21 and 22.

Recognition And Reunion In Heaven

In the Bible, David's infant son had just died. David made a statement about going to him someday, and obviously they will know each other.

> "He answered, while the child was still alive, I fasted and wept. I thought, Who knows? The Lord may be gracious to me and let the child live. But now that he is dead, why should I fast? Can I bring him back again? I will go to him, but he will not return to me."[69]

When the following people died, the Bible states that they were "gathered to their people." They went to be with their families, which was Hades in the Old Testament. After Jesus came and was resurrected the location changed to Heaven, therefore, everyone went to Heaven with Him.

---

[68] 1 John 2:24, NIV
[69] 2 Samuel 12:22-23, NIV

"Then Abraham breathed his last and died at a good old age, an old man and full of years; and he was gathered to his people."[70]

"Altogether, Ishmael lived a hundred and thirty-seven years. He breathed his last and died, and he was gathered to his people."[71]

"Then he breathed his last and died and was gathered to his people, old and full of years. And his sons Esau and Jacob buried him."[72] (This reference is about Isaac.)

"When Jacob had finished giving instructions to his sons, he drew his feet up into the bed, breathed his last and was gathered to his people."[73]

"Then the Lord said to Moses, Go up this mountain in the Abarim range and see the land I have given the Israelites. After you have seen it, you too will be gathered to your people, as your brother Aaron was."[74]

Jesus describes Heaven as a social place where people meet one another, enjoy themselves, and obviously recognize each other, as can be seen in this next verse.

"I say to you that many will come from the east and the west, and will take their places at the feast with Abraham, Isaac and Jacob in the Kingdom of Heaven."[75]

Richard Sigmund had some interesting things to say about what goes on in Heaven when people are about to arrive.

"People in Heaven knew they should be in the receiving area when someone is coming. Later I

---

[70] Genesis 25:8, NIV
[71] Genesis 25:17, NIV
[72] Genesis 35:29, NIV
[73] Genesis 49:33, NIV
[74] Numbers 27:12-13, NIV
[75] Matthew 8:11, NIV

learned there are announcement centers in Heaven, and people are notified that their loved ones were about to come to Heaven."

Sigmund, Richard. *A Place Called Heaven.*
Lightfall Publishing, 2004, Page 18.

"I walked by groups and groups of people and I could hear them talking. It was like the buzzing and busyness of people waiting at an airport or train station. They were obviously waiting for someone. And they were preparing something also."

"I heard people saying,'We did this because we knew he would like it.' 'Wait until he sees this.' It became obvious these people were involved in the preparation of a mansion. And it was a mansion for a member of their family. These groups were talking about a family member – a friend – who was about to arrive. And they had helped prepare his mansion for him."

Sigmund, Richard. *A Place Called Heaven.*
Lightfall Publishing, 2004, Page 71.

Communication In Heaven – Animal Talk

I wonder if it ever occurred to anyone that perhaps the animals were able to communicate with Adam and Eve in the Garden of Eden. Quite possibly animals spoke the same language as people before the fall. If that sounds unbelievable to you, allow me explain a little bit.

We know that some birds have the ability to talk, and they also deliver their responses at the appropriate time. Animals certainly understand our language, and they know what we're talking about. For instance, before I adopted my cat, Joey, who was a stray, I used to feed him in a certain place in our backyard. One day I told Joey that he could go up on the deck if he wanted to, and I pointed over to the deck. The very next day Joey was on the deck, and that was the first time he'd ever gone up there. My cat, Lukie, understands what I'm talking about when I tell him it's time to brush his teeth, and he starts running the other way. If you spend time around animals, you don't have to be convinced that they understand you; and while they don't respond verbally in our language, they do respond to us.

I've had a couple of dreams where two of my cats have spoken to me. It was terrific to be able to talk to them, even if it was only a dream. Unfortunately, I can't recall what their voices sounded like when they spoke.

You may have heard of Josephus Flavius (37–100 AD), a very well respected ancient historian. He was born into a family of priests, and he became a priest himself. In his writings called *The Antiquities Of The Jews*, Josephus makes the statement that "all the living creatures had one language."

He indicates that in the Garden of Eden, Adam and Eve communicated in the same language as all the animals. Josephus tells us that the lines of communication changed after Adam and Eve sinned. As you know, the beautiful, eternal, healthy, happy, and abundant life that God had planned for ***all*** of His creatures was altered after the fall. The serpent spoke with Eve, and told her that if she ate from the tree of knowledge of good and evil, they would not die. This was contrary to what God had told them. Eve and the serpent were communicating in the same language.

There's an interesting Bible story about a man named Balaam and his donkey from the book of Numbers. Balaam, a prophet of God, got into trouble because he disobeyed God by going someplace God didn't want him to go.

As he was riding along on his donkey one day, the donkey saw an angel standing in the road to block his way. At this point Balaam couldn't see the angel – only the donkey saw him! The donkey bolted off the road into a field, and Balaam started to beat the donkey for going off the road. Then the angel of the Lord stood at a place where the road narrowed between two vineyard walls. When the donkey saw the angel of the Lord standing there, he tried to squeeze by, and crushed Balaam's foot against the wall. So Balaam beat the donkey again. Then the angel of the Lord moved farther down the road, and stood in a place so narrow that the donkey could not get by at all. This time when the donkey saw the angel, he lay down under Balaam. In a fit of rage Balaam beat the donkey again with his staff.

Then the Lord caused the donkey to speak! "What have I done to you that deserves your beating me these three times?" the donkey asked Balaam. "Because you have made me look like a fool!" Balaam shouted. "If I had a sword with me, I would kill you!" "But I am the same donkey you always ride on," the donkey answered. "Have I ever done anything like this before?" "No," he admitted.

Then the Lord opened Balaam's eyes, and he saw the angel of the Lord standing in the roadway with a drawn sword in his hand. Balaam fell face down on the ground before him. "Why did you beat your donkey those three times?" the angel of the Lord demanded. I have come to block your way because you are stubbornly resisting me. Three times the donkey saw me and shied away; otherwise, I would certainly have killed you by now and spared the donkey." Then Balaam confessed to the angel of the Lord, "I have sinned. I did not realize you were standing in the road to block my way. I will go back home if you are against my going." But the angel of the Lord told him, "Go with these men, but you may say only what I tell you to say."[76]

To show you a similar case where God changed the speech of animals in the Garden of Eden, there's another story in the Scriptures about a change in languages for humans. The people were building a tower, called the Tower of Babel, and said they would go up into Heaven, and be like the most High. As a result, God changed the languages of the people into several different dialects so that they were unable to communicate with each other. Because of the different languages, the people were unable to communicate and work together on a project that God opposed. So we see an example of a time when God decided to alter our communication, and it remains this way today.

The disciple, John, saw a future vision of Heaven in the book of Revelation. He heard and saw all creatures praising God, including four special animal creatures that continually praise God around His throne. Clearly, John had to understand what all the animals were saying in order for him to state that all the creatures were praising God.

We already read Richard Sigmund's account that in Heaven there were horses that had the power of speech and he understood them. Also, Roberts Liardon's statement that he saw all kinds of animals. He said that there were birds of all sizes singing, and that they all seemed to be singing the same song. He said, "I found that I could understand what they were singing – there was no communication gap. When they

_____

[76] Numbers Chapter 22

stopped singing, it seemed as if they began to talk among themselves."

These are examples of how simple it is for God to give the power of speech to animals. I believe that someday in Heaven every creature that God has created will communicate perfectly with one another. I don't know what our pets will say to us when we're together in heaven, but it sure will be nice to have a two-way verbal conversation!

Will The Animals Be Included In The Rapture?

Yes, I believe they will be included in the rapture. The Scriptures in Romans 8:18-23 discuss the rapture of the body of Christ. In the following passages the animals are included.

> "Yet what we suffer now is nothing compared to the glory He will give us later. For all creation is waiting patiently and hopefully for that future day when God will resurrect His children. For on that day thorns and thistles, sin, death, and decay – the things that overcame the world against its will at God's command – will all disappear, and the world around us will share in the glorious freedom from sin which God's children enjoy."

> "For we know that even the things of nature, **like animals** and plants, suffer in sickness and death **as they await this great event**. And even we Christians, although we have the Holy Spirit within us as a foretaste of future glory, also groan to be released from pain and suffering. We, too, wait anxiously for that day when God will give us our full rights as His children, including the new bodies He has promised us – bodies that will never be sick again and will never die."

> Romans 8:18-23, The Living Bible [77]

---

[77] Romans 8:18-23, The Living Bible

Dr. Jack Van Impe has also stated that he believes that the animals will be included in the rapture in his DVD/video called *Animals In Heaven.* For those who do not know who Dr. Jack Van Impe is, here is some information about him.

Rev. Dr. Jack Van Impe is the President and Founder of Jack Van Impe Ministries International, Troy, Michigan. Dr. Jack Van Impe has been proclaiming the Word of God for over 50 years, and the Jack Van Impe Presents program that he co-hosts with wife, Rexella Van Impe, has had an astounding impact on our world. The fast-paced weekly TV program focuses on Bible prophecy, in which Dr. Van Impe is recognized as one of the leading experts in the world. Dr. Van Impe is renowned as "the walking Bible" because he has committed to memory nearly 10,000 verses of Scripture by subject – more than the entire New Testament. Dr. Van Impe is knowledgeable in virtually every area of Christian living, and is an avid student of Bible prophecy and world events. Several leading seminaries and Bible colleges across America have honored him with doctoral degrees in the field of theology.

For those who do not know what the Rapture is, I will explain. The rapture is an event whereby Jesus Christ will take Christians into Heaven. The Bible states that Jesus will not come all the way down to the earth, but will meet us up in the air. The Bible uses the term "caught up." It is an event that happens prior to the Second Coming of Jesus Christ (when Jesus does come down to earth). Here are some Scriptures on this subject.

> "Listen, I tell you a mystery: We will not all sleep (die), but we will all be changed — in a flash, in the twinkling of an eye, at the last trumpet. For the trumpet will sound, the dead will be raised imperishable, and we will be changed. For the perishable must clothe

itself with the imperishable, and the mortal with immortality."[78]

"For the Lord Himself will come down from Heaven, with a loud command, with the voice of the archangel and with the trumpet call of God, and the dead in Christ will rise first. After that, we who are still alive and are left will be caught up together with them in the clouds to meet the Lord in the air. And so we will be with the Lord forever."[79]

"For in the days before the flood, people were eating and drinking, marrying and giving in marriage, up to the day Noah entered the ark; and they knew nothing about what would happen until the flood came and took them all away. That is how it will be at the coming of the Son of Man. Two men will be in the field; one will be taken and the other left. Two women will be grinding with a hand mill; one will be taken and the other left."[80]

In this chapter we have studied the fact that "you're not dead when you die." All of God's creatures are triune beings, and it's only our bodies that die. When Jesus Christ comes back, our bodies will be resurrected. All born-again Christians, and all the animals will live in Heaven for eternity with the Lord.[81]

---

[78] 1 Corinthians 15:51-53, NIV
[79] 1 Thessalonians 4:16-17, NIV
[80] Matthew 24:38-41, NIV
[81] Psalm 36:6, Romans 8:18-23

Chapter 5

Overcoming Depression

The duration of the grieving and healing process is different for everyone. Making efforts to recover from a mourning period does not mean that you have forgotten your pet or that you are being disloyal to them. Please know that I care about what you are going through, and that's why I wrote this book as well as ***There Is Eternal Life For Animals.*** The Bible tells us to mourn with those who mourn, and this is what all Christians should do whether they are animal lovers or not.[82] "Praise be to the God and Father of our Lord Jesus Christ, the Father of compassion and the God of all comfort, who comforts us in all

---

[82] Romans 12:15

our troubles, so that we can comfort those in any trouble with the comfort we ourselves have received from God.[83]

While depression during this time is natural, try to move back into a normal, healthy, and emotionally balanced lifestyle as soon as possible. In order to do that, we have to start with our thoughts. How you channel your thoughts will determine the outcome of your well being, as well as your families. Thoughts of our loss will continue to go through our minds; however, we can decide what to do with those thoughts. We can choose not to be sad and depressed.

When you begin to think of something sad, redirect your thoughts in a positive way. I think that a big key to the survival of pet loss is "thinking Heaven." The Bible says to set our affections on things above, and the Amplified Bible says to think on "the higher things."[84]

Something that helped me during the mourning process, along with Bible research on animals going to Heaven, was reading books by Christian authors who went to Heaven during near-death or out-of-body experiences. I have made a list of these books at the end of this chapter, and they may help you, as well. While these books are not as the authority of God's Word, they are confirmations of what the Bible teaches about Heaven and eternal life.

My recommendations are: 1) Seek God and His ways of healing, 2) Concentrate on Heaven and our future together, and 3) Keep busy doing good for others, perhaps helping animals.

When we help others we are blessed, and it will help to take our minds off ourselves.[85] There are many ways that you can help animals. Here are some suggestions:

- Adopt another pet.

---

[83] 2 Corinthians 1:3-4, NIV
[84] Colossians 3:2
[85] Acts 20:35

- Join a pet prayer group.

- Pray for animals everywhere.

- Volunteer to help at animal shelters. Perhaps you could walk a dog.

- Donate money and needed supplies to animal shelters. Sometimes local stores collect food for shelters, and you can just drop something in the box on your way out.

- Sign petitions to stop any kind of animal cruelty, and to promote the well being of animals.

- Give somebody and their pet a ride to their veterinarian's office if they don't have transportation.

- Join a pet support group. Your knowledge on a particular subject may help others.

- Join a feline Trap Neuter Release (TNR) group to successfully manage cat colonies.

- Feed the birds in your yard – they love sunflower seeds. This helps chipmunks and squirrels, too.

- Report animal abuse to your local Humane Society.

- Spay and neuter your own pets.

- Keep your cats indoors and your dog on a leash or in a fenced in yard. They will be safer and will live longer, healthier lives.

- Leave funds in your will to support the care of any pets you may leave behind, and you could also leave funds for a good animal organization. There's a book that you might find helpful on this subject called *When Your Pet Outlives You* by David Congalton and Charlotte Alexander.

*"And if you spend yourselves in behalf of the hungry
and satisfy the needs of the oppressed,
then your light will rise in the darkness,
and your night will become like the noonday."*

Isaiah 58:10, NIV

Think About Heaven

Begin to think that they must look wonderful in Heaven. They are more handsome or beautiful than ever. Perhaps much like they were in the prime of their lives. They are, no doubt, having a wonderful time. Think about how good you feel that they are not sick any more, and that there are no dangers in Heaven. They must be playing with all the other animals, which are at peace with each other. They're having a fantastic time, which is not to say that they don't miss us, but I'm sure they wouldn't come back if they could. Why? Because it has to be too wonderful in Heaven to want to leave, and they know it's just a matter of time until you arrive there and you're reunited with them.

I find myself thinking that Pete must be running around in our mansion, and thinking that it's a really cool place. I can picture him running around corners flying in the air like they do in the cartoons. He always loved grass, and there's plenty of delicious grass in Heaven for him to munch on. I think he's hanging out with my Dad, and they're sometimes talking about me.

I was brought up in a good Christian home where we prayed and read the Bible, so I think Pete is telling my Dad about all the times I prayed for him. I would anoint him with oil, and sometimes use a prayer cloth from an anointed minister.[86] After hearing this, my Dad is really impressed that all his hard

---

[86] Acts 19:11-12

90

work in teaching me about the Lord has paid off. I can hear Dad right now saying to Pete, "is that right?" Then Pete turns to Dad and says, "How do you like Heaven?" and my Dad using an expression with an Englishman's accent as he always did, says, "It's a bit of alright."

I think Pete would be going for a ride on an elephant. I think he's saying that Mommy told me I'd be coming here someday, and now I can't wait until she joins us, along with my Dad and brother, Lukie.

Your dog is probably playing ball, riding on a horse or running through a lovely field. Try to use your imagination to visualize exactly what you think is happening in Heaven. Then put a smile on your face, and say, they're having a blast!

We need to pray that the Lord will help us through our difficult times whatever they may be. The Lord is available 24/7. He's always ready and waiting to hear from us. You'll never call Heaven and get a recording that says: I'm away from the throne right now, but your call is important to Me. Please leave your name, telephone number, and a detailed message, and I'll call you right back." No, God always hears our prayers, and He cares about us.[87] The Lord loves us and He is always near.[88] God is bigger than any problem or depression you may have, so tell your problems how big your God is! "But blessed is the man who trusts in the Lord, whose confidence is in Him."[89] Overcoming hardship is impossible for us, but with God all things are possible.[90] Putting our hope in God will not disappoint us, because God has poured out His love into our hearts.[91]

You can pray and ask the Lord to give you peace regarding your beloved animal companion being healthy, happy, and safe

---

[87] I Peter 5:7
[88] John 3:16, Psalm 145:18
[89] Jeremiah 17:7, NIV
[90] Matthew 19:26
[91] Romans 5:5

in Heaven. Here are a couple of sample prayers that may help you.

Dear Lord,

[Pet's name] is in Heaven, and I must face a time of separation until the day that we are reunited with them. Please comfort me and soften the pain during our temporary separation. Help me to think positive and good thoughts that will be pleasing to You, and beneficial to me. Help me to be a real blessing to as many of Your creatures as possible while I am here on earth. We ask this in Jesus Name.

Amen.

Dear Lord,

Please bring me peace and a great hope of seeing [pet's name] in Heaven someday. Soften the pain of this difficult loss. We know that Your Word says in Psalm 36:6 that God preserves people and animals, and we believe You when You say that You are preserving them in Heaven throughout eternity. May the peace and anticipation of their reunion with us in Heaven someday bring a better quality of life to us. This we ask in the name of the Father, the Son, and the Holy Spirit.

Amen.

Why Did My Pet Have To Die?

I want to make sure you know that God does not put sickness on His creatures. He wants all of us to be well. If you look at the life of Jesus and His ministry, you will see that He spent the majority of His time healing people of their sicknesses.[92] He also said that if you have seen Me, you have seen The Father, meaning God The Father and God The Son, Jesus, both agree on everything that He was doing.[93] This tells us very plainly and clearly that God does not put sickness on us, and He does not want any of His creatures to be sick.

So where does sickness come from? It comes from the Devil, also called Satan or Lucifer. The Bible says, "How God anointed Jesus of Nazareth with the Holy Spirit and power, and how **He went around doing good and healing all who were under the power of the devil**, because God was with Him.[94] "The thief (meaning Satan) comes only to steal and kill and destroy; I have come that they may have life, and have it to the full."[95] So if your pet was hurt in some way, it didn't come from God – it came from Satan.

Sickness and death never were in God's plan for His creation. It exists in our lives only because Adam and Eve disobeyed God. Thus, the need for a Savior – Jesus Christ.

Bishop LaDonna Osborn says in her book, ***God's Big Picture***, that there are four dynamic events of redemption:

1. God's Creation,

2. Satan's Deception,

3. Christ's Substitution, and

4. Our Restoration.

---

[92] Matthew 4:23-24, Luke 4:40, and Matthew 14:14
[93] John 14:9
[94] Acts 10:38, NIV
[95] John 10:10, NIV

Dear Lord,

Thank you for the precious opportunity to share Your love and compassion with others today. I know that as I step out to give of myself, You will use me to be a blessing to others, and I will be healed.

Amen.

If You Have A Pet Who Is Sick

If you are reading this book and you have a pet that is currently sick, I would encourage you not to give up. The Bible says that God is a rewarder of those who diligently seek Him.[96] Familiarize yourself with what the Bible teaches on prayer, faith, and healing, and believe God for a miracle! I would recommend my book, *Animal Prayer Guide*, as it goes through the Scriptures on this subject, and gives you good prayer examples that you can customize to suit your own needs.

We take prayer requests for animal companions on our website www.eternalanimals.com. As a result of finding that there are so many sick pets, I wrote the book *Animal Prayer Guide* to help people pray more effectively for their animal companions. I was amazed at how many sick pets there were.

We needn't wait until our pets are sick to pray for them. The time to start praying for them is from day one, but it's never too late too start.

I realize that we all will die some day, unless Jesus comes back for the rapture first, but we need to be aware that He came that we would have life to the full, or as the King James Version translation reads, to have life more abundantly.[97]

We are thankful that our cat, Pete, lived to be 21 years old. Of course, I would have liked him to live much longer, however that is considered a long life for a cat. We prayed and prayed over Pete innumerable times throughout his life, and we are thankful to God for every minute we had with him!

Thinking Positive Thoughts

The Bible tells us what to think about for a healthy mind, soul, spirit, and body. It says, "Whatever is true, noble, right, pure, lovely, and admirable — if anything is excellent or

---

[96] Hebrews 11:6
[97] John 10:10

praiseworthy — think about such things."[98] The Amplified Bible says to "fix your mind on them." "You will keep in perfect peace all who trust in You, all whose thoughts are fixed on You! Trust in the Lord always, for the Lord God is the eternal Rock."[99] Right thinking will change your outlook, and bring healing.

God has given us a sound mind,[100] and that means living a healthy and happy life. "A happy heart makes the face cheerful, but heartache crushes the spirit."[101] "A cheerful heart is good medicine, but a crushed spirit dries up the bones."[102] The Bible tells us to have the mind of Christ or to think like Him.[103]

Words produce thoughts, and thoughts create the feelings that dwell up in you. They can be your own words or those of other people. For instance, if you watch something sad or depressing in a movie or on TV, it will produce thoughts that can have a negative impact on you. In other words, guard your emotions, particularly during this sensitive time. I'm not saying that you shouldn't have a good cry, especially in the beginning, but then you have to pull yourself up by your bootstraps, and work toward your healing. You have to get away from the clutches of Satan, because he wants to keep you depressed. You are in a temporary trial,[104] but God heals the broken in heart and binds up their wounds.[105]

Here are a couple of sample prayers that you can use to help you to think positive.

---

[98] Philippians 4:8, NIV
[99] Isaiah 26:3-4, NIV
[100] 2 Timothy 1:7
[101] Proverbs 15:13, NIV
[102] Proverbs 17:22, NIV
[103] 1 Corinthians 2:16, Philippians 2:5
[104] 1 Peter 1:6
[105] Psalm 147:3

Heavenly Father,

I commit my thoughts to You today. I purpose in my heart to stay focused on You, and the good plan You have for me. Holy Spirit, remind me of God's Word so I can fill my heart with His promise of victory today. We pray in the Name of Jesus.

Amen.

Dear Heavenly Father,

I thank You for this day. Teach me how to think like You, and see myself the way You see me, so I can experience all You have for me today. Remove all feelings of depression and sadness, and fill me with the joy of the Lord. In Jesus Name.

Amen.

Finding Strength and Joy In Praising God

A good way to overcome sadness is to praise God even when we don't feel like it, and He will give us strength for our healing. " For the joy of the Lord is your strength."[106] When people in the Bible were in trouble, they found the victory in praising God. One example is when Paul and Silas were put in prison.

"About midnight Paul and Silas were praying and singing hymns to God, and the other prisoners were listening to them. Suddenly there was such a violent earthquake that the foundations of the prison were shaken. At once all the prison doors flew open, and everybody's chains came loose."[107]

The Lord said that He would be with us throughout all of our troubles and suffering.[108] He is the source of kindness, understanding, and comfort.[109] Here are some additional Scriptures to help you.

"I will extol the Lord at all times; His praise will always be on my lips. My soul will boast in the Lord; let the afflicted hear and rejoice. Glorify the Lord with me; let us exalt His name together. I sought the Lord, and He answered me; He delivered me from all my fears. Those who look to Him are radiant; their faces are never covered with shame."

"This poor man called, and the Lord heard him; He saved him out of all his troubles. The angel of the Lord encamps around those who fear Him, and He delivers them. Taste and see that the Lord is good; blessed is the man who takes refuge in Him."[110]

---

[106] Nehemiah 8:10, KJV
[107] Acts 16:25-26, NIV
[108] Isaiah 43:2
[109] 2 Corinthians 1:3
[110] Psalm 34:1-8, NIV

"Now is your time of grief, but I will see you again and you will rejoice, and no one will take away your joy."[111]

"God is our refuge and strength, a very present help in trouble."[112]

"For in the time of trouble He shall hide me in His pavilion: in the secret of His tabernacle shall He hide me; He shall set me up upon a rock."[113]

We can find comfort and strength in the Lord and His Word if we discipline our minds to believe what God says. We need to stay consistent and focused in our thinking. We can overcome depression, and look forward to our reunion with our beloved animal companions in Heaven. We can do all things through Jesus who gives us strength. [114]

---

[111] John 16:22, NIV
[112] Psalm 46:1, KJV
[113] Psalm 27:5, KJV
[114] Philippians 4:13

Recommended Books About Heaven

Springer, Rebecca Ruter. *My Dream Of Heaven*: A Nineteenth Century Spiritual Classic. Tulsa: Harrison House, 2002, ISBN: 1577944704.

This is a reprint of **Intra Muros,** Rebecca Ruter Springer, David C. Cook Publishing Company, 1898. This is the book that tells the stories about the little girl being reunited with her kitten, and Rebecca seeing a dog she once had.

Baker, H. A. *Visions Beyond The Veil: God's Revelation to Children of Heaven and Hell.* Gabriel Resources, 2002. (There are various printings of this book). Also from Whitaker House, ISBN numbers: 0883684012, 1973, and 1852402784, 2006.

Davis, Marietta. *Scenes Beyond The Grave* Edited by Gordon Lindsay. Christ For The Nations, 1990, ISBN: 089985091X.

Duplantis, Jesse. *Heaven: Close Encounters Of The God Kind.* Tulsa: Harrison House, 1996, ISBN: 0892749431.

Hagin, Kenneth E. *I Believe In Visions.* Tulsa: Faith Library Publications, 1996, ISBN: 0892765089.

Sigmund, Richard. *A Place Called Heaven.* Lightfall Publishing, 2004, ISBN: 1888398183.

Van Impe, Jack. *Animals In Heaven*. DVD/Video.

Chapter 6

Look To The Future

Fluffy's In Heaven

I'm sad every day, I cry and I mourn;
Little Fluffy, my love, it seems he's gone home;
I can't see this place that's waiting for me;
The scene that's in Heaven, enchanting, you see;
Angels flying above, and the trumpets they sound;
Beautiful gardens, flowers, and paths all around;
Clearest rivers and lakes, and the streets made of gold;
The lion and lamb are asleep, while the birds sing and tweet;
People laugh and talk as they stroll in the breeze;
Grandpa golfs on the lawn, children play on the swings.

Fluffy and friends tour the mansion for me;
They race through my house, up the stairs joyfully;
Sliding down the banister, right on their rears;
Taking corners so fast they can fly through the air;
In the kitchen they slide across a bright shiny floor;
Eating snacks they do feast by the patio door;
So happy, no troubles, no tears anymore;
Everything so perfect, but just one thing more;
When reunited in Heaven, we'll live happily evermore!

Niki Behrikis Shanahan

How is this Paradise possible for us all? Over 2,000 years ago in a humble manger with all the animals surrounding Him, the greatest event in the history of the world took place. The birth of Jesus Christ. He is the author and finisher of our faith, and He is the reason that all creatures have a future. The Apostle Paul said,

> "I consider that our present sufferings are not worth comparing with the glory that will be revealed in us."[115]

Paul is saying that compared to the eternal happiness we will have, our troubles will fade behind us.

In the book of Titus it says,

> "A faith and knowledge resting on the hope of eternal life, which God, who does not lie, promised before the beginning of time."[116]

We can count on God to do what He said He'd do. He said He'd have a home for us in Heaven if we'll live for Him, and all the animals will be there.

God's big picture is the same as His original plan, which started in the Garden of Eden. His resolve is that He isn't going to abandon His plan for our good, happy, and blessed future.

When we speak of eternal life, exactly what does eternal mean? It means endless or limitless time, having an infinite duration, everlasting, and never ending! Jesus said whoever lives and believes in Me shall never die.[117] This means we die once, (unless Jesus comes back for the rapture of His people and animals, Romans 8:18-23) we're resurrected, and then we live forever together. In the books of Hosea and Peter it says:

> "I will ransom them from the power of the grave; I will redeem them from death. Where, O death, are your

---

[115] Romans 8:18, NIV
[116] Titus 1:2, NIV
[117] John 11:26, NIV

plagues? Where, O grave, is your destruction?"[118] "O death, where is thy sting? O grave, where is thy victory?"[119]

"Praise be to the God and Father of our Lord Jesus Christ! In His great mercy He has given us new birth into a living hope through the resurrection of Jesus Christ from the dead, and into an inheritance that can never perish, spoil or fade — kept in Heaven for you, who through faith are shielded by God's power until the coming of the salvation that is ready to be revealed in the last time."

"In this you greatly rejoice, though now for a little while you may have had to suffer grief in all kinds of trials. These have come so that your faith — of greater worth than gold, which perishes even though refined by fire — may be proved genuine and may result in praise, glory and honor when Jesus Christ is revealed. Though you have not seen Him, you love Him; and even though you do not see Him now, you believe in Him and are filled with an inexpressible and glorious joy, for you are receiving the goal of your faith, the salvation of your souls."[120]

... There is hope for your future,"
declares the Lord ...

Jeremiah 31:17, NIV

---

[118] Hosea 13:14, NIV
[119] 1 Corinthians 15:55, KJV
[120] 1 Peter 1:3 – 9, NIV

Bill and Gloria Gaither wrote a song called, ***Because He Lives***. Here are some of the words that describe why we can look to the future.

God sent His Son – they called Him Jesus,

He came to love, heal and forgive;

He lived and died to buy my pardon,

An empty grave is there to prove my Savior lives.

Because He lives I can face tomorrow,

Because He lives all fear is gone;

Because I know He holds the future;

And life is worth the living just because He lives.

And then one day I'll cross the river,

I'll fight life's final war with pain;

And then, as death gives way to victory,

I'll see the lights of glory – and I'll know He lives.

My husband, Jack, my beloved cats, Pete, Lukie, Joey, and I look forward to meeting all of you and your beloved animal companions in Heaven someday!

"Looking unto Jesus the author and finisher of our faith ..."

Hebrews 12:2, KJV

Chapter 7

Memorial Service

*"For He shall give His angels
charge over thee ..."*

Psalm 91:11, KJV

A memorial service can be done at any time, not just at the time of your beloved animal companion's passing. There are many ways to remember your beloved animal companion. When shopping, the infant sections are a good place to look for such items. Special photos in lovely frames are comforting to have around you. I bought a large collage frame that has the word "baby" on it, and filled it with photos of my beloved cat, Pete. I mixed the photos up so that most of them are just Pete, and others are one with Mom, one with Dad and one with his brother, Lukie.

In fact, after I did Pete's collage, I liked it so much that I did one for Lukie, too. You don't have to wait until they go to Heaven to celebrate their life! I made their own special photo albums, and again, the baby sections work out good because you can find lovely photo albums with Noah's ark and other animals on them.

I also bought a white porcelain cross container which I used to store locks of Pete's hair, whiskers, his nails and his ID tag. I used to save little locks of his hair when it came off, and I would put it in an envelope for the day when we would have to temporarily part.

I recommend that you read my book called *There Is Eternal Life For Animals.* It will bring you great comfort as you study the Scriptures, which reveal that all animals go to Heaven. Your beloved animal companions are not only in your past – they are in your future!

"Blessed are they that mourn:
for they shall be comforted."

Matthew 5:4, KJV

... *"For I will turn their mourning into joy,*
and will comfort them,
and make them rejoice from their sorrow."

Jeremiah 31:13, KJV

The Memorial Service

We are confident, I say, and willing rather
to be absent from the body,
and to be present with the Lord.

II Corinthians 5:8, KJV

You can include anything personal you may wish to say. For song suggestions, see the Bibliography section.

Prayer In A Memorial Service

Dear Lord,

We commit into Your hands this day Your loving creature, [name]. We ask that [name's] joy would be full in [his/her] new home in Heaven. Please reunite us with [name] when we get to Heaven ourselves, and bless us with an eternity together. Thank you for the life of this beautiful animal. Thank you for the privilege of enjoying so many months and years of friendship and companionship with Your dear creature. In Jesus' name we pray.

Amen.

Bible Readings

God Giving Life

"And God said, 'Let the land produce living creatures according to their kinds: livestock, creatures that move along the ground, and wild animals, each according to its kind.' And it was so. God made the wild animals according to their kinds, the livestock according to their kinds, and all the creatures that move along the ground according to their kinds. And God saw that it was good."[121]

God's Blessing In Life

"The Lord is my shepherd; I shall not want. He maketh me to lie down in green pastures: He leadeth me beside the still waters. He restoreth my soul: He leadeth me in the paths of righteousness for His Name's sake. Yea, though I walk through the valley of the shadow of death, I will fear no evil: for Thou art with me; Thy rod and Thy staff they comfort me. Thou preparest a table before me in the presence of mine enemies: Thou anointest my head with oil; my cup runneth over. Surely goodness and mercy shall follow me all the days of my life: and I will dwell in the house of the Lord for ever."[122]

---

[121] Genesis 1:24-25, NIV
[122] Psalm Chapter 23, KJV

The Lord Comforts Us

"The Lord is close to the brokenhearted and saves those who are crushed in spirit. A righteous man may have many troubles, but the Lord delivers him from them all."[123]

"I will lift up mine eyes unto the hills, from whence cometh my help. My help cometh from the Lord, which made Heaven and earth."[124]

"As for me, I will call upon God; and the Lord shall save me. Evening, and morning, and at noon, will I pray, and cry aloud: and He shall hear my voice."[125]

"Come to me, all you who are weary and burdened, and I will give you rest."[126]

"So with you: Now is your time of grief, but I will see you again and you will rejoice, and no one will take away your joy."[127]

"Praise be to the God and Father of our Lord Jesus Christ, the Father of compassion and the God of all comfort."[128]

Jesus Made Eternal Life Possible

"For God so loved the world, that He gave His only begotten Son, that whosoever believeth in Him should not perish, but have everlasting life."[129]

"Jesus said to her, 'I am the resurrection and the life. He who believes in Me will live, even though he dies;

---

[123] Psalm 34:18-19, NIV
[124] Psalm 121:1-2, KJV
[125] Psalm 55:16-17, KJV
[126] Matthew 11:28, NIV
[127] John 16:22, NIV
[128] 2 Corinthians 1:3, NIV
[129] John 3:16, KJV

and whoever lives and believes in Me will never die. Do you believe this?'"[130]

"Let not your heart be troubled: ye believe in God, believe also in Me. In My Father's house are many mansions: if it were not so, I would have told you. I go to prepare a place for you. And if I go and prepare a place for you, I will come again, and receive you unto Myself; that where I am, there ye may be also. And whither I go ye know, and the way ye know. Thomas saith unto Him, Lord, we know not whither Thou goest; and how can we know the way? Jesus saith unto him, I am the Way, the Truth, and the Life: no man cometh unto the Father, but by Me."[131]

"For since by man came death, by man came also the resurrection of the dead. For as in Adam all die, even so in Christ shall all be made alive."[132]

The Resurrection of Christ

"Now, brothers, I want to remind you of the gospel I preached to you, which you received and on which you have taken your stand. By this gospel you are saved, if you hold firmly to the word I preached to you. Otherwise, you have believed in vain."

"For what I received I passed on to you as of first importance: that Christ died for our sins according to the Scriptures, that He was buried, that He was raised on the third day according to the Scriptures, and that He appeared to Peter, and then to the Twelve. After that, He appeared to more than five hundred of the brothers at the same time, most of whom are still living, though some have fallen asleep."

---

[130] John 11:25-26, NIV
[131] John 14:1-6, KJV
[132] I Corinthians 15:21-22, KJV

"Then He appeared to James, then to all the apostles, and last of all He appeared to me also, as to one abnormally born. For I am the least of the apostles and do not even deserve to be called an apostle, because I persecuted the church of God. But by the grace of God I am what I am, and His grace to me was not without effect. No, I worked harder than all of them – yet not I, but the grace of God that was with me. Whether, then, it was I or they, this is what we preach, and this is what you believed."[133]

God Preserves People and Animals

"Thy righteousness is like the great mountains; Thy judgments are a great deep: O Lord, Thou preservest man and beast."[134]

"Thou, even Thou, art Lord alone; Thou hast made Heaven, the Heaven of Heavens, with all their host, the earth, and all things that are therein, the seas, and all that is therein, and Thou preservest them all; and the host of Heaven worshippeth Thee."[135]

The Resurrection Of The Animals With Us

"Yet what we suffer now is nothing compared to the glory He will give us later. For all creation is waiting patiently and hopefully for that future day when God will resurrect His children. For on that day thorns and thistles, sin, death, and decay – the things that overcame the world against its will at God's command – will all disappear, and the world around us will share

---

[133] I Corinthians 15:1-11, NIV
[134] Psalm 36:6, KJV
[135] Nehemiah 9:6, KJV

in the glorious freedom from sin which God's children enjoy."

"For we know that even the things of nature, **like animals** and plants, suffer in sickness and death **as they await this great event**. And even we Christians, although we have the Holy Spirit within us as a foretaste of future glory, also groan to be released from pain and suffering. We, too, wait anxiously for that day when God will give us our full rights as His children, including the new bodies He has promised us – bodies that will never be sick again and will never die."[136]

"The Lord hath made bare His holy arm in the eyes of all the nations; and all the ends of the earth shall see the salvation of our God."[137]

"Then shall the dust return to the earth as it was, and the spirit shall return unto God who gave it."[138]

The Resurrection of the Dead

"But if it is preached that Christ has been raised from the dead, how can some of you say that there is no resurrection of the dead? If there is no resurrection of the dead, then not even Christ has been raised. And if Christ has not been raised, our preaching is useless and so is your faith."

"More than that, we are then found to be false witnesses about God, for we have testified about God that He raised Christ from the dead. But He did not raise Him if in fact the dead are not raised. For if the dead are not raised, then Christ has not been raised either. And if Christ has not been raised, your faith is futile; you are still in your sins. Then those also who

---

[136] Romans 8:18-23, The Living Bible
[137] Isaiah 52:10, KJV
[138] Ecclesiastes 12:7, KJV

have fallen asleep in Christ are lost. If only for this life we have hope in Christ, we are to be pitied more than all men."

"But Christ has indeed been raised from the dead, the firstfruits of those who have fallen asleep. For since death came through a man, the resurrection of the dead comes also through a man. For as in Adam all die, so in Christ all will be made alive. But each in his own turn: Christ, the firstfruits; then, when He comes, those who belong to Him. Then the end will come, when He hands over the kingdom to God the Father after He has destroyed all dominion, authority and power. For He must reign until He has put all His enemies under His feet. The last enemy to be destroyed is death. For He 'has put everything under His feet.'"

"Now when it says that "everything" has been put under Him, it is clear that this does not include God Himself, who put everything under Christ. When He has done this, then the Son Himself will be made subject to Him who put everything under Him, so that God may be all in all."[139]

Is your beloved animal companion still alive? Yes! As you read the next Scriptures, note that it says, "If there is a natural body, there is also a spiritual body." The Apostle Paul is speaking about the bodies of mankind and the bodies of animals!

The Resurrection Body

"But someone may ask, "How are the dead raised? With what kind of body will they come?" How foolish! What you sow does not come to life unless it dies. When you sow, you do not plant the body that will be,

---

[139] I Corinthians 15:12-28, NIV

but just a seed, perhaps of wheat or of something else. But God gives it a body as He has determined, and to each kind of seed He gives its own body."

"All flesh is not the same: **Men have one kind of flesh, animals have another, birds another and fish another.** There are also Heavenly bodies and there are earthly bodies; but the splendor of the Heavenly bodies is one kind, and the splendor of the earthly bodies is another. The sun has one kind of splendor, the moon another and the stars another; and star differs from star in splendor."

"So will it be with the resurrection of the dead. The body that is sown is perishable, it is raised imperishable; it is sown in dishonor, it is raised in glory; it is sown in weakness, it is raised in power; **it is sown a natural body, it is raised a spiritual body.**"

"If there is a natural body, there is also a spiritual body. So it is written: "The first man Adam became a living being;" the last Adam, a lifegiving spirit. The spiritual did not come first, but the natural, and after that the spiritual."

" The first man was of the dust of the earth, the second man from Heaven. As was the earthly man, so are those who are of the earth; and as is the man from Heaven, so also are those who are of Heaven. And just as we have borne the likeness of the earthly man, so shall we bear the likeness of the man from Heaven. I declare to you, brothers, that flesh and blood cannot inherit the kingdom of God, nor does the perishable inherit the imperishable."

"Listen, I tell you a mystery: We will not all sleep, but we will all be changed – in a flash, in the twinkling of an eye, at the last trumpet. For the trumpet will sound, the dead will be raised imperishable, and we will be changed. For the perishable must clothe itself with the imperishable, and the mortal with immortality."

"When the perishable has been clothed with the imperishable, and the mortal with immortality, then the saying that is written will come true: "Death has been swallowed up in victory." "Where, O death, is your victory? Where, O death, is your sting?" The sting of death is sin, and the power of sin is the law. But thanks be to God! He gives us the victory through our Lord Jesus Christ."[140]

The Future Told In The Book Of Revelation

"And every creature which is in Heaven, and on the earth, and under the earth and such as are in the sea, and all that are in them, heard I saying, Blessing, and honour, and glory, and power be unto Him that sitteth upon the throne, and unto the Lamb for ever and ever."[141]

"And I saw an angel standing in the sun; and he cried with a loud voice, saying to all the fowls that fly in the midst of Heaven, Come and gather yourselves together unto the supper of the great God."[142]

Jesus Will Dry Our Tears

"And I heard a loud voice from the throne saying, 'Now the dwelling of God is with men, and He will live with them. They will be His people, and God Himself will be with them and be their God. He will wipe every tear from their eyes. There will be no more death or

---

[140] I Corinthians 15:35-57, NIV
[141] Revelation 5:13, KJV
[142] Revelation 19:17, KJV

118

mourning or crying or pain, for the old order of things has passed away.'"[143]

"There is no death!
What seems so is transition:
This life of mortal breath
Is but a suburb of the life elysian,
Whose portal we call death."

Longfellow

---

[143] Revelation 21:3-4, NIV

Joining Our Animal Companions In Heaven

If you are not sure that you are ready to go to Heaven, you can commit your life to Jesus Christ today. Also, by doing so you will be able to spend eternity with your beloved pet!

A commitment to Christ requires a step of faith, an acceptance of the sacrifice, which He made for you. By dying on the Cross for us, Jesus has washed our sins clean with His blood.

Bible Readings

"If we confess our sins, He is faithful and just to forgive us our sins, and cleanse us from all unrighteousness."[144]

"That if you confess with your mouth, "Jesus is Lord," and believe in your heart that God raised Him from the dead, you will be saved. For it is with your heart that you believe and are justified, and it is with your mouth that you confess and are saved."[145]

"Therefore being justified by faith, we have peace with God through our Lord Jesus Christ."[146]

If you are ready to make that commitment, and if you want to say "Yes" to Jesus, then say the following prayer out loud:

Dear Jesus,

Thank you for the sacrifice You made for me. I am sorry for my past sins, and will try my best not to repeat them. I ask Your help to keep this pledge. I know I am not worthy but I willingly accept You as my Lord and Savior, and I thank You for Your blessing over my family and me. Please make me ready today to make Heaven my eternal home. Thank you that today I am born again. Amen.

---

[144] I John 1:9, KJV
[145] Romans 10:9-10, NIV
[146] Romans 5:1, KJV

Bibliography

Shanahan, Niki Behrikis. *There Is Eternal Life For Animals.* Tyngsborough: Pete Publishing, 2002, ISBN: 0972030107.

Shanahan, Niki Behrikis. *Animal Prayer Guide.* Tyngsborough: Pete Publishing, 2005, ISBN: 0972030123.

Booth, General William. *Visions.* London: The Salvation Army Printing Works, 1906.

Baker, H. A. *Visions Beyond The Veil:* God's Revelation to Children of Heaven and Hell. Gabriel Resources, 2002.

Davis, Marietta. *Scenes Beyond The Grave.* Edited by Gordon Lindsay. Christ For The Nations, 1990.

Atwater, P.M.H., Lh. D. *Children Of The New Millennium.* Three Rivers Press, 1999.

Duplantis, Jesse. *Heaven: Close Encounters Of The God Kind.* Tulsa: Harrison House, 1996.

Springer, Rebecca Ruter. *Intra Muros.* David C. Cook Publishing Company, 1898.

You may be interested in reading a reprint of *Intra Muros*, which is called *My Dream Of Heaven:* A Nineteenth Century

Spiritual Classic, Rebecca Ruter Springer. Tulsa: Harrison House, 2002, ISBN: 1577944704.

Neils, Jenifer and Oakley, John H. Hanover: *Coming Of Age In Ancient Greece, Images of Childhood from the Classical Past.* Yale University Press, 2003.

Cansdale, G. S. *All The Animals Of The Bible Lands.* Zondervan Publishing House, 1970.

Wood, Rev. J. G. *Story Of The Bible Animals.* Philadelphia: Charles Foster Publishing Co., 1888.

Lindsay, Gordon. *Death And The Hereafter.* Christ For The Nations, 1978.

Lindsay, Gordon. *Life After Death.* Christ For The Nations, 1988.

Van Impe, Jack. *Animals In Heaven.* Jack Van Impe Ministries, DVD/Video.

Osborn, LaDonna. *God's Big Picture.* Osborn Publishers, 2001.

Hagin, Kenneth E. *I Believe In Visions.* Tulsa: Faith Library Publications, 1996, ISBN: 0892765089.

Sigmund, Richard. *A Place Called Heaven.* Lightfall Publishing, 2004, ISBN: 1888398183.

Liardon, Roberts. *We Saw Heaven.* Tulsa: Insight Publishing Group, 2000, ISBN: 1890900-24-9. This book includes the books by Marietta Davis, H. A. Baker, and Rebecca Ruter Springer. The Rebecca Ruter Springer section, however, does not include her seeing a pet cat and dog as some versions of her book have omitted this. For the complete book, which includes the story about the dog and cat, see *My Dream of Heaven:* A Nineteenth Century Spiritual Classic, Rebecca Ruter Springer, Harrison House, 2002, ISBN: 1577944704.

Congalton, David and Alexander, Charlotte. *When Your Pet Outlives You.* NewSage Press, 2002, ISBN: 0939165449.

Hymns Of Glorious Praise. Springfield: Gospel Publishing House, 1969.

Hymn references:

I Sing The Mighty Power Of God, Isaac Watts

Amazing Grace, John Newton

All Creatures Of Our God and King, Saint Francis of Assisi

This Is My Father's World, Maltbie D. Babcock

King James Version, referred to as KJV, B. B. Kirkbride Bible Co., Inc., 1964.

New International Version, referred to as NIV, Zondervan Bible Publishers, 1978.

The Living Bible, A. J. Holman Company, 1973.

New King James Version, referred to as NKJV, Thomas Nelson Publishers, 1982.

There Is Eternal Life For Animals
A Book Based On Bible Scripture
By Niki Behrikis Shanahan

As you read this book you will discover that:

- Our pets do go to Heaven.

- There are people who have actually seen pets and animals in Heaven.

- The Bible tells us that there are animals in Heaven.

- God loves and cares for the animals.

- Animals have souls and spirits.

- Animals are included in God's redemption plan.

- Accurate translations of the original Greek and Hebrew words make it even clearer that the promise of eternal life is for all of creation.

"I have just finished reading the book, and feel that it was well done."

Rev. Dr. Jack Van Impe, Michigan

"I read your book, and it opened my eyes to a whole other realm. Keep up the good work!"

Frederick K. C. Price, D.D.
Founder & Pastor of
Crenshaw Christian Center, California

"Excellent, Outstanding and Life Changing!"

Rev. Shirley Johnson, Florida, MidWest Book Review

"It is a privilege to recommend 'There Is Eternal Life For Animals.'"

Rev. Dr. Peter Hammond, South Africa
Founder & Director of Frontline Fellowship
and Africa Christian Action

Animal Prayer Guide
A Book Based On Bible Scripture
By Niki Behrikis Shanahan

Experience The Power Of God In Prayer!

- A guide to praying for animals with sample prayers, which can be personally customized.
- A Blessing of the Animals Service, Memorial Service, and Pet Dedication.
- Accounts of answered prayers, Bible readings, and Scriptural truths on receiving answers to prayer.
- Heartwarming anecdotes & fascinating Bible stories.
- Delightful photos to make you smile.

We recommend ***Animal Prayer Guide*** so that you will understand the Scriptures pertaining to prayer, faith, and the promises of God. Spiritual knowledge translates into physical blessings when we activate the Word of God. By studying the Bible Scriptures you will increase your knowledge of God, and learn how prayer and healing can work for you and your animal companion. We are always happy to pray for your pet, but everyone needs to learn how to call on God for help 24/7.

"My prescription: provide good food and exercise,
see your veterinarian for yearly exams
and use the prayers in this wonderful book."
Amanda Oden Corliss, DVM, Massachusetts

"Questions answered and backed-up by Scripture, sample
prayers to help you along the way, and encouragement to
never give up can all be found within the pages of this book."
Rev. Shirley Johnson, Florida, Senior Reviewer, MidWest Book Review

"Filled with numerous true stories of wit
& wisdom in equal parts,
Niki's second book is a pure delight."
Annie Mals, President, The Peaceful Kingdom Alliance 4 Animals, California

About The Author

Niki Behrikis Shanahan is the author of *There Is Eternal Life For Animals* and *Animal Prayer Guide.* She has a very unique Christian animal ministry. Niki donates much of her time in grief counseling for pet owners, and in praying for sick and lost animal companions.

Niki is the Founder of Pete Publishing, and she is a member of the Cat Writer's Association (CWA). She is the creator of www.eternalanimals.com, and maintains the website.

She is from New England and is married to Jack Shanahan. They have two handsome cats, Luke and Joey. Her very special cat, Pete, currently resides in Heaven.

We hope that this book has been beneficial and comforting to you. Please feel free to write to us. We'd like to know if this book has helped you!

You may order additional copies of *The Rainbow Bridge: Pet Loss Is Heaven's Gain*, as well as *There Is Eternal Life For Animals* and *Animal Prayer Guide* in print or E-Book form by visiting us at www.eternalanimals.com or contact the publisher at the following address:

Niki Behrikis Shanahan
Pete Publishing
P. O. Box 282
Tyngsborough, MA 01879

Email: eternalanimals@comcast.net

We welcome you to visit us at:

www.eternalanimals.com

Our website is dedicated to animals and pets with a focus on animal afterlife from a Christian perspective, prayer for pets, and animal appreciation. You'll find articles, stories, news, health and wellness information, photos, and other resources. We welcome prayer requests for animals.

God Bless You And Your Family!